Getting from Paycheck to Paycheck— Simply

Getting from Paycheck to Paycheck —Simply

by

Barbara Horak

BEACON HILL PRESS OF KANSAS CITY
Kansas City, Missouri

ISBN: 0-8341-0780-5

Printed in the United States of America

Cover by: Royce Ratcliff
Illustrated by: Keith Alexander

All scriptures quoted, unless otherwise designated, are from the *New International Version.*

Dedication

This book is dedicated to

Charlie

Exciting husband,
Devoted father,
Honest provider,
A big guy with a gentle heart.

Acknowledgments

I am indebted to Mrs. Roberta Walker for her patience and interest in proofreading and editing early drafts; to Rev. Henri Pol and Joseph S. Johnson for their comments and suggestions; and to the editors at Beacon Hill Press of Kansas City who edited the manuscript for publication.

Contents

Foreword

That the love of money is the root of all evil is axiomatic. But one need not worship at this golden shrine to encounter problems. The mismanagement of money can be an open road to embarrassment, frustration, strife, and disruption of marital harmony.

Christian stewardship involves consecration of material possessions to God. Good stewardship is carefully planned, prayerful, informed management of one's income.

Money management is not an isolated theme. Books and pamphlets are advertised in most magazines and found on the shelves of every bookstore. Barbara Horak's book is distinctive in that it is written from a Christian point of view.

The author is a professional—a certified public accountant. She is versed in accounting and as a homemaker and mother of three, understands the subtleties of impulsive spending, credit card financing, and the importance of planning and record keeping in family budgeting.

Young people contemplating or beginning marriage will find in the following pages directions for planned spending with occasional bits of advice on matters related to victorious Christian living.

The book has been written in answer to a real need. I am sure Mrs. Horak was prompted by the Holy Spirit to undertake this substantial task.

—Leon D. Doane
Vice-president, Head Office
Idaho First National Bank
Boise, Idaho

Getting from Paycheck to Paycheck—Simply

INTO EVERY LIFE A LITTLE RAIN MUST FALL
BUT THIS IS RIDICULOUS!

1

Managing Our Money

The first time I took the rigorous, three-day Certified Public Accountant's exam, one fact became obvious to me—none of the fellow applicants had ever seen an eight-months-pregnant woman in that circumstance before. A year later, I received my certificate—five months pregnant with our third child.

Much has happened these last 13 years. The first 9 years, I practiced public accounting in El Paso, Tex., specializing in income taxes. These last 4 years I have been officially the vice-president and secretary of my husband's general contracting corporation. In reality, and more down to earth, I have been the tax consultant, bookkeeper, payroll and accounts payable clerk, receptionist, and typist for this multi-million-dollar corporation.

But my work in the business world has always been part time! The first priority in my life is being a wife and mother. Being a Christian, of course, spreads out like an umbrella to cover all these activities.

The last two years I have had a real concern for the many Christians who are burdened with financial worries. Where I have done counseling in money management or have led money management seminars, I have found that financial worries and problems generally stem, not from lack of finances, but from lack of money management skills.

How do *you* stack up as a money manager? If you need help, join the crowd. The truth is, we probably all have a great deal to learn in becoming more effective money managers, a problem that seems to be universal. According to the American Bar Association, 72 percent of divorces have financial problems as their root cause. Two out of five families have debt problems, according to a Federal Reserve Board report.

There are some very good reasons why many are doing a miserable job of managing their finances. Lack of education, in my estimation, is at the top of the list. We spend 10, 12, or even 16 years in school getting an education aimed mainly toward the goal of earning money. Think about how much time you have spent in education aimed at managing that money. Probably none!

Our education has made it easier for us to earn money than to manage it wisely. This situation led one person to exclaim in exasperation, "We are illiterate when it comes to personal financial management."

I repeat, there are some very good reasons why we are doing a miserable job of managing our finances. But there is no good reason why we should continue to do such a lousy job! This is not a situation we are likely to outlive, so we might as well sit down and resolve to do something about it—NOW. I mean *really* resolve to do something about it. Wouldn't you rather be in the driver's seat, choosing the route, than being taken for a ride? You can be! It can be fun!

Many times Jesus talked about money. He told 38 parables, 16 of which dealt with money and our attitudes toward money. I have searched the Scriptures and find that God's Word has much to say to us about our assets and liabilities. It's no secret to God that money is very important to us; we don't have to be ashamed of this feeling. If you are a Christian, you have a distinct advantage in money matters over nonbelievers. You've got God in your corner of the ring.

I love to talk about money.

But money has its limitations. We can't eat it, live in it, or wear it. Benjamin Franklin said, "The use of money is all the advantage there is in having it." Did you get that? Having money is to no advantage; using money is where the action is. Therein lies the importance of management. *Of what use is money in the hand of a fool, since he has no desire to get wisdom?* (Prov. 17:16).

We must first recognize our need and then be willing to develop management skills that will enable us to use our money *wisely*.

There are over 1 billion adults living now who are not able to read this book and over 2 billion adults who do not have the resources to buy such an item. If you purchased and are able to read this book, you have more material wealth than most in the world can even imagine, and you have been blessed with an education beyond the wildest dreams of many. In other words, we are rich—rich by comparison and rich by definition! And God expects a lot from us. *From everyone who has been given much, much will be demanded; and from the one who has been entrusted with much, much more will be asked* (Luke 12:48).

Do you recall the story that Jesus told in Matthew 25 about the master who left three servants in charge of his assets while he was away? The lesson we sometimes miss in this familiar parable of the talents is this: The master required an accounting immediately on his return. We have been entrusted with the use of God's assets, and we'd better believe we are going to have to make an accounting for them! Will you be able to do this?

PAY ME!
BALANCE ME!

2

We've Got to Get Organized

The fact is, we are all money managers.

The question is, are we *good* money managers?

The answer is, we probably could all be more effective.

We can identify with the person who prayed, "Lord, either quiet the waves or lift me above them. It's too late to learn to swim!"

If you feel as if you're drowning in money problems, relax; it's *never* too late to learn to swim. I know many people are struggling just to stay afloat financially. This idea is substantiated in such books as *Money Talks, It Says Good-bye,* by Bill King, and *It Only Hurts Between Pay Days,* by Amy Ross Young.

Money management is an area easy to neglect. It is an area we *want* to do something about, we *intend* to do something about, but *put off* doing anything about it. It's hard to know where to start. The fact that you are reading this book indicates you are serious about doing something NOW.

We will start simply, and gradually work toward the goal of actually being in control of our situation. We'll learn to tread water before we tackle the strokes that will enable us to make headway. Before too long we'll be able to go a whole lap.

Your Advantage as a Christian

If you are a Christian, you have the additional incentive of God's promise to help: "Commit to the Lord whatever you do, and your plans will succeed" (Prov. 16:3).

God loves it when we turn our impossible situation over to Him. He wants so badly to help us, to support us, and to give us a joyful, abundant, and exciting life. It must break His heart to see our misery as we agonize over our financial problems, especially when He knows this is so unnecessary.

Money cannot buy happiness, though. It can relieve tension and bring happiness if other areas of our lives are in proper perspective and if our priorities are straight; in other words, if we have put God first, and have managed wisely what He has given us.

You *can* get help from God for your financial problems, for He loves to take good care of His children. If you are not a Christian, you can become one, because God's arms are wide open to welcome you into His family. Salvation, life's greatest treasure, is not available at any price. It is free.

Growing in understanding as a Christian comes in part from reading the Bible, so as a basis for this study, I suggest that you read your Bible regularly. I personally prefer a modern translation. As you read, ask God to reveal himself to you through His Word. He will! Also find a place to worship and be faithful in attending. Being with other Christians is important to one's steady growth, for mutual encouragement strengthens all of us.

One of the benefits of being a child of God is that all of His promises are available to those who walk with Him. He has promised to answer prayer, to meet our needs, and even to give us the desires of our hearts. He will help you work out your financial problems if you commit your life to Him sincerely, with determination to do His will.

Let's commit this whole effort to Him right now, in prayer:

Lord, I know You do not want me burdened with financial concerns. I ask Your help in dealing with my problems, and ask Your guidance in developing a plan that will work for me. I pray this in the name of my Lord, Jesus Christ, as I seek to do Your will. Amen.

You now have God's guarantee of success. As you proceed, continue to ask Christ to have an active voice in your planning and decisions. Let Him help with the nitty-gritty details of everything from balancing your checkbook to saving for your vacation. He wants to help! He will help!* (But don't forget to thank Him!)

Live Within Your Income

There is a fact of life that seems never to have entered the consciousness of many: we must live within our income.

Read that again! We must live within our income! We need to reorganize our expenditures to match our paycheck, rather than always looking for ways to make more money to cover our expenditures. Instead of focusing on living with what we have, we are constantly trying to figure out how to have more. With the instinct of lemmings, droves of people rush into credit buying as one solution.

We cannot long survive living beyond our means, because at some point forces outside our control will work to limit our ability to spend more than we make. Creditors will not allow us to continue the practice of using now and paying later (which, by the way, is called *debt*) when we are not able to keep our promise to pay promptly. As the very drastic consequences of our being unwilling to live within our income, our purchases will be repossessed if we are unable to meet our obligations, and in some states

*See Appendix for supporting scripture.

creditors can take part of our wages before we ever see our paycheck.

Our federal government has given us the bad example of not living within its income. Its answer to making more money is, literally, printing more. As in individuals, governmental overspending is indicative of immaturity and discontent.

Keep It Simple

You have spent a lot of time learning how to make money, and even more time and sweat earning it. Now let's spend the next few hours developing skills for managing all that hard-earned cash. Our password to success—SIMPLE. Evaluate each procedure by this password. If it isn't the simplest possible way to accomplish your goal, think of a simpler, easier way.

Let's Get Started

Here's what we're going to do. First, we will get into the nuts and bolts of a simple, easy system of recording expenditures. We need this information put together in such a way that we can easily see what our money was spent for. I will suggest a worksheet that you can use to record your money plan, as well as for recording one whole year of expenditures. To compile this type of record will probably take approximately one hour per month. (More about recording expenditures in the next chapter.)

After that we will discuss step by step how to make a money plan that can be fun and exciting.

In other chapters, we will discuss ways to get our money's worth; the prosperity God intends for us; possible reasons we're not experiencing prosperity; the dangers of wealth; Christmas spending that can be disastrous; the dangers and blessings of credit, and how to get a misshapen financial situation into shape using principles of weight control. We'll also look at what the Bible says about work. The Appendix can be a valuable tool, so don't overlook it. It contains a list, by subject, of Bible passages dealing with money matters.

The ideas in this book will help you develop skills that will allow you to:

1. Organize your financial affairs so that you will, in fact, be able to live within your means—and live very nicely at that.

2. Determine how you will spend and on what. You can be in control of where your money goes.

3. Reach financial goals. Where you go from here really is your decision.

4. Reduce careless spending! Have you ever said, "I don't know how I could do any better; I buy only the bare necessities as it is." Ideas in Chapter 4, "She really is good at spending money!" will help in this area.

5. Provide for family needs (not just necessities—such as a $2,000 orthodontist's fee, a $45.00 dress for a beauty contest or a $650 vacation).

As you read this book, I expect you to start developing fresh, new, creative ideas in dealing with money. This venture can be both fun and exciting. Don't continue to do something just because "that's the way it's always been done." Do some original thinking! Be innovative! Approach your money matters with a new, better attitude—and anticipate miracles.

What have you got to lose? Anxiety, worry, frustration.

What have you got to gain?

1. Satisfaction in knowing you are in control of your financial situation.
2. Security in knowing where you are and where you are going.
3. The buoyant feeling of knowing you're doing a good job.
4. A more abundant life.

I DO REALIZE YOUR MONEY PROBLEMS ARE SERIOUS, DAVID,... BUT DULL.

3

Be Original

The way I see it, Christians have a certain advantage over nonbelievers—thanks to God's forgiveness. Our minds don't have to be cluttered with the guilt, worry, and anxiety over unforgiven sin, which means we should be able to think more clearly. The unforgiven person has a whole garbage pail of sins to struggle with constantly. But even though we have this advantage, don't let pride tell us, "I won't forget," or "I don't need to write that down." Let's face it: we all forget, and forgetfulness is not necessarily a result of age. We will see as we write down our monthly expenditures, our debts, our goals, and our money plans—see them in black and white—that the actual process of recording will help free us from some of the nagging worries of our money situation.

As you begin, you will need three things:

1. The desire to succeed;
2. An adding machine, and
3. A pad of columnar paper.

It is hard for me to visualize a person working without an adding machine, but if you are one of those mathematical geniuses I've never had the pleasure to meet, go ahead without one. You can buy a pad of work paper at any office supply store for approximately $3.00. Be sure to get paper with 14 columns, a description space, and at least 50 lines. These pads come in different colors, so pick a color to match your eyes, or your adding machine, or something equally important. We will use this same work paper for all the schedules, as well as for other uses I will suggest.

I have also found it helpful to have a comfortable place to work, such as a desk or work table. And quiet—a luxury we don't always have. I can accomplish more between 10 p.m. and midnight, after the children are in bed, than at any other time. But you work out the best place and time for you.

Each person has a different level of effectiveness already established, so if some points seem too elementary for you, rejoice and bear with us; there'll be something you can use later on.

We have already established the magic word, SIMPLE. There are all sorts of elaborate schedules that you can use in your record keeping. But it has been my experience that many of these require too much time and, consequently, after a few months they are not maintained. So I suggest the following simple schedules that require a minimum of time to prepare:

1. Expenditures worksheet, posted each month.
2. Estimate of income, prepared once each year.
3. Unpaid bills, prepared once each year.
4. Goals worksheet, prepared each year and updated as needed.
5. Money plan, prepared once each year.

We will discuss schedules 2, 3, 4, and 5 in the next chapter.

Expenditures Worksheet

Our first step is to try to get a handle on where our money has been going. To record our expenditures, we need the simplest, easiest way—which still gives us the information we need. On the next page is the format for a worksheet to record a whole year of expenditures, as well as your money-plan guidelines. Column 1 will be used to record your money-plan guidelines; columns 2 through 13 will be used to record each month's expenditures; and column 14 will be used for the year's total. These annual totals will be valuable as you work out your money-plan guidelines for the coming year. As you look at this worksheet, "think original." If it won't work for you, change it. Or make your own format.

There is a very important money-management rule I would like to inject here: MAKE ALL PAYMENTS BY CHECK. When you pay with a check, you record in your check register or on your check stub, the date, the payee, and the amount. *Presto,* you have the equivalent of a cash disbursement record. Without realizing it, you are doing what bookkeepers get paid to do. You have every expenditure in black and white (hopefully not red). And at the end of each month, it will not be necessary to strain the brain to remember where that wad of cash went.

Some families have more than one checking account for varying reasons. I prefer only one for a very simple reason—I hate reconciling the bank statement. It's enough to have to reconcile one account each month.

Now, let's take a closer look at the expenditures worksheet. See following page.

Notice the description column as I have set it up. There are some line items you may not need. If you rent, you wouldn't use house insurance and real estate taxes on line 4. If you don't own a car, you wouldn't need the detail under car expenses on lines 11, 12, and 13. You can use these lines for other items such as condo maintenance payments, furniture, car pool expenses, employee expenses, child care and expenses generated by a self-employed person.

Here's a fast way to accumulate your expenditures each month. Start with the first item on the worksheet. Take your check register or stubs and quickly scan for

Expenditures Worksheet

		Money Plan Guideline	Jan.	Feb.	Mar.
	Housing: Payment or Rent				
	Utilities & Telephone				
	Maintenance & Other				
	Insurance & Taxes				
30%	Total Housing				
17%	Food				
10%	Tithe				
	Auto: Gas				
	Ins., Repairs, License				
8%	Total Auto				
5%	Insurance: Life & Med.				
	Debt Payments: Credit Cards				
	Installments				
	Auto				
	Loans				
8%	Total Debt Payments				
4%	Clothing				
5%	Savings				
2%	Medical Expenses				
	Entertain. & Recreation				
	Eating Out				
	Vacations				
	Babysitters				
	Other				
5%	Total Entertain. & Recreation				
	Other: Beauty & Barber Shop				
	Allowances				
	Lunches				
	Books, Subscriptions				
	Gifts (Incl. Christmas)				
	Music Lessons				
	Education Expenses				
6%	Total Other				
	Total Expenditures				
	Income: Salaries, Take-Home				
	Other				
	Total Income				

Expenditures Worksheet

		Money Plan Guideline	Jan.	Feb.	Mar.
	Housing: Payment or Rent	$ 318			
	Utilities & Telephone	115			
	Maintenance & Other	20			
	Insurance & Taxes				
30%	Total Housing	453			
17%	Food	260			
10%	Tithe	217			
	Auto: Gas	120			
	Ins., Repairs, License	36			
8%	Total Auto	159			
5%	Insurance: Life & Medical	24			
	Debt Payments: Credit Cards	18			
	Installments	57			
	Auto	173			
	Loans	-0-			
8%	Total Debt Payments	248			
4%	Clothing	46			
	"Surprise"	30			
5%	Savings	46			
2%	Medical Expenses	70			
	Entertainment & Recreation:				
	Eating Out	43			
	Vacations	8			
	Babysitters	13			
	Other	6			
5%	Total Entertain. & Rec.	70			
	Other: Beauty & Barber Shop	6			
	Allowances	13			
	Lunches	22			
Set aside in Svg.	Books, Subscriptions	—			
	Gifts (Incl. Christmas)	42			
	Music Lessons	30			
	Education Expenses	-0-			
6%	Total Other	112			
	Total Expenditures	$ 1723			
	Income: Salaries, Take-home	$ 1511			
	Other	212			
	Total Income	$ 1723			

amounts paid out for that item. As you find these amounts, run an adding machine tape of them and mark each amount as you add it, with a check mark (✔). Total the amounts in the machine and enter that total on the correct line on the worksheet. Now go to the next line item and accumulate the amounts paid in the same way. Do this for each item on your worksheet.

When you think you have entered every amount from your checkbook somewhere on the worksheet, go back through to see if there is a check mark by each amount—to make sure you didn't miss any.

If you made expenditures that are not recorded in your checkbook—dig out the receipts, grocery tapes, or whatever. Arrive at totals for these items and enter them on the proper line. If you haven't kept these, estimate how much you spent. Remember in the future to keep this information on purchases or payments not made by check. Have an envelope or a file folder in a handy place where you can stick these receipts and tapes until the time you are ready to prepare your worksheet.

Some items, such as car insurance, college tuition, estimated income tax payments, and some insurance premiums, are paid quarterly, semiannually, or annually. You need to be aware of these payments, and I suggest you enter an amount each month equal to one-twelfth of the annual amount, even though you will not make a payment in that particular month. Allocating these expenses in this way will give more meaningful monthly totals.

Now you are ready to total your expenditures and enter the amount on line 45. This total can be shocking, so brace yourself.

Next enter your take-home pay on line 47, any other income on lines 48 and 49; then give the total of these income items on line 50. Other income will include only amounts actually received during the month, such as interest, dividends, proceeds from a garage sale, self-employment income, and so on.

Now sit back in a comfortable chair and study the information you have just accumulated. How does your total income, line 50, compare with your total expenditures, line 45? Favorably, I hope. Do any of your figures leap off the paper at you? The first month I kept this worksheet, the huge amount we spent for eating out made me so nauseous that we didn't eat out for the next two weeks!

After you have your money-plan guidelines recorded in column 1 (the steps in organizing your plan will be covered in the next chapter), compare the guidelines to your actual expenditures. Are you on target, or way off base?

This whole procedure of recording expenditures should take only 30 minutes to one hour. If accumulating the information this first month seemed confusing, I guarantee that next month you will be able to do it in half the time and with half the effort. Do not wait till January to start using this worksheet. Start with whatever month you're in now.

There is another feature of this worksheet that may be of value to you. In the far left-hand column are some percentages. These figures are provided as a guideline to compare against your money plan and your actual monthly expenditures. The value of these percentages is limited by the fact that there is no "average family." Such a creature does not exist and never will. The Bureau of Labor Statistics defines an "average family" as consisting of two parents, two children (none of whom is in college), a certain income (it changes each year), and no major medical problems.

Of course, a family making $15,000 will spend a larger percentage of their income on food and shelter than a family making $36,000. But even though limited, these percentages might still be helpful just for comparison. For example, if you are having to spend 30 percent of your income on debt service (payments to reduce existing debts), maybe you need to do something about that.

To summarize a bit, your worksheet provides, in black and white, a record of where your money has gone. You can use your figures to formulate your own money plan and to compare with that plan. The worksheet also lets you see what priorities our spending habits have established—these might not necessarily be the priorities you intended.

If the format or form of the worksheet didn't work well for you, did you change it? For example, on our worksheet we've had to add a line item for Girl Scout cookies, which has become a significant expenditure. You may need to do the same.

Isn't it exciting studying your expenditures, written out all nice and neat? Doesn't it make you feel secure because you know exactly where your money went last month, and now you don't have to wonder about it? Isn't it fun looking forward to next month, knowing how much better you're going to do in your money management?

ONE MILLION
AFTER TAXES
HOME
SWEET
HOME

4

A Cruise to Tahiti?

Estimate of Income

The next step is to estimate your annual income in order to see what you have available to spend. A simple schedule for accumulating your income information is illustrated on the following page. You can put this schedule on the same kind of work paper. Start with your gross salaries (salaries before deductions). If you have more than one salary, list each one and enter the total on line 5. Do not anticipate and record a raise, unless it is absolutely certain and you are sure what date it will become effective.

Next, list all deductions from your pay. Besides income and social security taxes, other deductions might include state income tax, health or life insurance premiums, union dues, retirement-plan contributions, employee association fees, etc. Assuming these deductions are taken out of *each* check, here is an easy way to figure the annual amount of your deductions. Look at the stub from your last paycheck and multiply each deduction by the number of pay periods in a year. If you are paid weekly, multiply by 52; biweekly, multiply by 26; semimonthly, multiply by 24; or monthly, by 12. If the deductions are taken out only once a month and you are paid weekly (for example) the amount will need to be prorated.

Suppose you are paid biweekly, and the following items are deducted from *each* paycheck:

Income tax (sometimes called withholding tax)	$130.80
Social security (sometimes called F.I.C.A.)	$55.17
Health insurance premiums	$12.15

The amount of annual deductions is calculated as follows:

ESTIMATE OF INCOME:	1	2	3	4	5
		1980		1981	
GROSS SALARIES					
Star Electronics		$ 21840 00		$ 23400 00	
TOTAL SALARIES		21840 00		23400 00	
LESS DEDUCTIONS					
Income Taxes	$ 3008 20		$ 3400 80		
Social Security Taxes	1338 74		1556 10		
Other: Health Insurance	315 90		315 90		
		4662 84		5272 80	
NET INCOME FROM SALARIES (Take-home Pay)		17177 16		18127 20	
OTHER INCOME:					
Self Employment Income		1800 00		2100 00	
Interest		412 50		450 00	
Dividends		-0-		-0-	
Other		-0-		-0-	
TOTAL ANNUAL EXPENDABLE INCOME		$ 19389 66		$ 20677 20	
TOTAL MONTHLY EXPENDABLE INCOME (÷ 12)		$ 1615 80		$ 1723 10	

Income tax	$130.80 × 26 = $3,400.80
Social security	$55.17 × 26 = $1,434.40
Health insurance	$12.15 × 26 = $315.90

Enter the annual total of all paycheck deductions and subtract them from total salaries to arrive at net income from salaries (take-home pay).

Now list other income. Estimate self-employment income at net (income less related expenses). Unless there has been a large change in the amount of your savings or investments, interest and dividends can be estimated using your prior year's figures. These two figures can be found on your prior year's federal income tax return. Other income might include social security benefits, scholarship funds, gifts, royalties, and unemployment compensation. Anything else? List it. Add these items of other income to your net income from salaries to arrive at your total *annual* expendable income. Convert your *annual* income to *monthly* income by dividing by 12 and enter this amount on line 24.

Now you can see what you have to work with. I hope you are pleasantly surprised. Does it amount to more than you realized? Was your first reaction, "Where has it all gone?" If so, this should strengthen your resolve to do a better job of managing all that money, because let's face it, it's not all that easy to come by!

Unpaid Bills

We live in an age of credit buying—it has become a way of life. In the later chapter, "Credit—Privilege or Curse?" we will take a closer look at the pitfalls and dangers, as well as the blessings, of using credit.

For our purposes now, we need to get a handle on just how much of our monthly income is needed for our debt payments, and for how long. The simple schedule of unpaid bills (see next page) can also be put on the same kind of work paper we have been using. All debts, except your home mortgage, need to be listed. These might include installment purchases, home improvement loans, car loans, medical bills, and any other debts that you intend to pay out over a period of more than one month. This debt information will probably be on a purchase agreement, sales contract, or monthly statement. If you are in doubt, call your creditor and ask. Do *not* list debts that will be paid within a month—such as department store charges, utility bills, gasoline credit card charges, etc. Notice this one worksheet can be used for as many years as there is space.

You might want to add other information columns, such as the amount of finance or interest charges and amount of original indebtedness. Again, remember—keep it SIMPLE. Record only that information that will be useful to you, and do it in the easiest way. After you have listed your debts, total column 2, total amount owing now, and column 3, monthly payment required.

UNPAID BILLS:	1	2	3	4	5
OWING TO	DATE INCURRED	TOTAL AMT. OWING YOU	MONTHLY AMT. REQUIRED	DATE TO BE PAID OFF	FINANCE CHARGES
AT 12/15/79					
Sears (sewing machine)	6/79	$175.00	$30.00	6/80	18%
Dept. Store (revolving chgs.)	various	549.00	25.00	10/81	18%
VISA (furniture)	12/79	836.00	40.00	9/81	18% on $500 12% on rest
Bank (car)	3/79	4660.47	172.61	3/82	11.96%
		$6220.47	$267.61		
AT 11/30/80					
Dept. Store (revolving chgs)	various	$389.00	$85.00	3/82	18%
VISA (furniture)	12/79	356.00	18.00	9/82	18%
Bank (car)	3/79	2589.15	172.61	3/82	11.96%
Dr. Stevens	9/80	389.00	50.00	8/81	-0-
		$3723.15	$265.61		

If you think you might be overextended, filling out a worksheet such as this can be the first step in dealing with the problem. We'll say more about that later in the chapter on "Financial Dieting."

Goals Worksheet

Now for the best part! Sit back. Relax. Start to dream. Think about all the things you want to do; all the things you want to accomplish; all the places you want to go; all the joys of retirement you want to have. Let the sky be the limit! Jot down your ideas. Direct your dreaming in terms of what you want to do or accomplish this year; within five years; and beyond five years. This process might take several days and might involve the whole family. But if you are married, husband and wife must work together as a team. Everyone involved should make individual notes; then all the family members should sit down together and discuss them. Throw in something that seems extravagant. Maybe you've always dreamed of two weeks at a luxurious health spa or a cruise to Tahiti. With proper advance planning, you can make almost any dream happen.

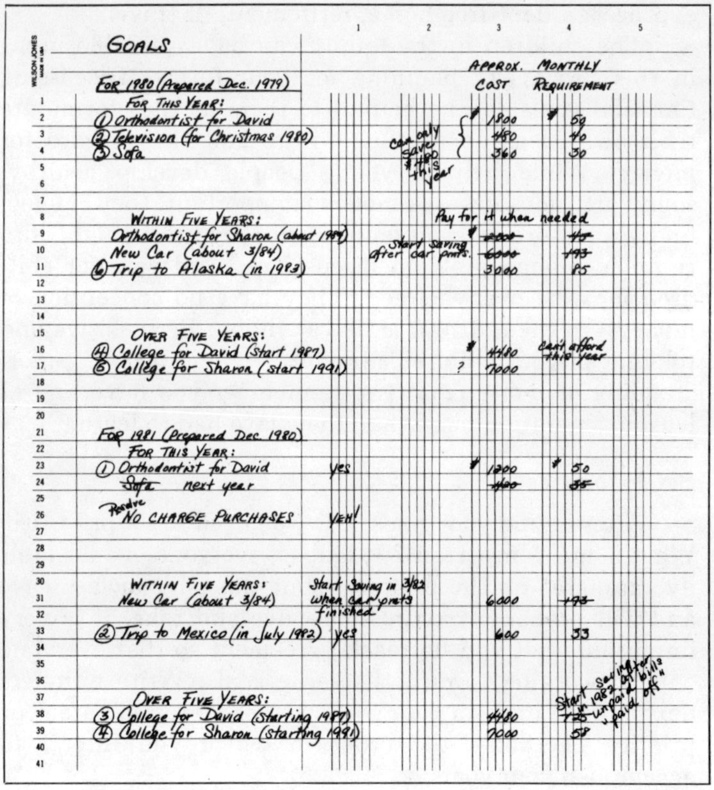

GOALS		Approx. Cost	Monthly Requirement	
For 1980 (Prepared Dec. 1979)				
For This Year:				
① Orthodontist for David	can only save $480 this year	$ 1800	$ 50	
② Television (for Christmas 1980)		480	40	
③ Sofa		360	30	
Within Five Years:		Pay for it when needed		
Orthodontist for Sharon (about 1984)		$ ~~2000~~	~~45~~	
New Car (about 3/84)	start saving after car pmts.	~~6000~~	~~193~~	
⑥ Trip to Alaska (in 1983)		3000	85	
Over Five Years:				
④ College for David (start 1987)		$ 4480	can't afford this year	
⑤ College for Sharon (start 1991)	?	7000		
For 1981 (Prepared Dec. 1980)				
For This Year:				
① Orthodontist for David	yes	$ 1200	$ 50	
~~Sofa~~ next year		~~400~~	~~35~~	
Resolve No Charge Purchases	YEH!			
Within Five Years:				
New Car (about 3/84)	Start Saving in 3/82 when car pmts finished	6000	~~193~~	
② Trip to Mexico (in July 1982)	yes	600	33	
Over Five Years:				Start Saving in 1982 after "unpaid bills" paid off
③ College for David (starting 1987)		4480	~~125~~	
④ College for Sharon (starting 1991)		7000	58	

As you get your thoughts together about your future, list your dreams on a schedule such as the one on page 25.

Your goals for this year, for example, might include a new washing machine, reducing or paying off your unpaid bills, building up a savings fund for emergencies or beginning piano lessons. Within the next five years you may want to plan for the down payment on a house, braces for the children's teeth, increased giving to the church, a new car or a vacation to Florida. Your long-range goals, over five years, may also include such items as college education expenses, a debt-free home, retirement, or travel.

The children in the family can have valuable input in this process of planning for your future. Discussing financial goals can be helpful to them as they formulate their own ideas about their future and their regard for money. While helping young people develop healthy, sound attitudes towards money is important, they can feel undue pressure or even guilt when they are brought into complex money problem discussions. And younger children may be overwhelmed. They have no conception of money—to them $1,000 is like a trillion. Be sensitive and tolerant of your children's immaturity and lack of understanding of money matters. Remember you have had at least a generation more than they have had to learn.

Set Priorities

After listing your goals, now you need to set priorities. What is most important? It helps if everyone in your family can agree on the priorities, but this isn't always easy and will probably require some give and take. It is very important that you do reach agreement so that everyone will be working toward the same goals. Write numbers next to each item on your goals worksheet to indicate your priority decisions—the order in which you intend to accomplish your goals.

These priorities might change from time to time; and in fact, some goals that seem important to you today might seem ridiculous just one year from now. You need to be willing to change your strategy as your circumstances change. Put a date on your "Goals" worksheet, and each time you add to it, take items off, or change your priorities, make a note of the date you made such changes. Over the years there will be many changes, and you will find it interesting to see when these changes took place and why. You will probably want to make a new "Goals" worksheet at least once each year (probably at the time you are formulating your money plan for a new year). Use the same sheet of work paper and use several other columns; this way you can get five or six years of goals on one worksheet.

Determine Costs

Now you need to estimate the cost of each goal. For example, if you wish to provide a college education for a child who is now in seventh grade, you need to work through a calculation such as this:

Time to prepare	6 years	
Type of college	Out-of-town, but in home state	
Cost for one year, at today's prices:		
Tuition & fees		$ 300
Books and supplies		200
Room & board		1,400
Airfare home, twice		300
Other		600
		$2,800
Approximate cost in six years: $2,800 × 1.60 = (Assuming 10 percent rate of inflation per year)		$4,480

Through the calculation you can see the cost of four years college to be approximately $17,920 ($4,480 × 4). Of course, you are making some assumptions that may or may not prove to be true, but at least you have a place to start. As circumstances change (rate of inflation, cost of tuition, possibility of scholarships, etc.), you can adjust your figures.

If you decide you would like to have at least one-half of the total available at the time your little darling is ready to join the campus scene, then you will need to start saving $125 each month right now. This is calculated as follows:

Total cost for 4 years	$17,920
Divide by 2 to arrive at ½ of cost	÷ 2
One-half of total cost, rounded off	= $9,000
Number of years to prepare	÷ 6
Savings required each year	= $1,500
To calculate monthly requirement	÷ 12
Savings required each month	= $125

Also keep in mind that there will be accumulated interest on the money deposited.

In determining the cost of longer term goals, you will need to consider many variables, but go ahead and give these calculations your best effort. Your planning is flexible, so you can make changes later, as needed.

Money Plan

Now you are ready to determine how you intend to use your money in the future—and the future starts right now. You have in black and white where you have been (Expenditures Worksheet); what you have to work with (Estimate of Annual Income); your present obligations (Unpaid Bills); and what you want to achieve (Goals). These are your tools to work out your very own money plan.

List the same items as you used on your Expenditures Worksheet on a work paper, such as the one illustrated on page 28. Use pencil as you'll probably have to erase and redo several times before you arrive at the plan with which you are happy. Keep your Expenditures, Unpaid Bills, and Goals worksheets in front of you as you consider each item of your money plan. If you have not recorded your expenditures for at least two months, go back and do this.

Taking one item at a time, decide what amount you intend to spend on it in the coming year. For example, your "Housing Payment or Rent" can easily be determined by multiplying the required monthly amount by 12. This is an area of fixed expense with no leeway short of moving your household to another locale. The next item, "Utilities and Telephone," is flexible enough to allow for some savings through positive decisions on your part. For example, you may resolve to conserve on gas, water, and electricity; or to write more letters and make fewer long-distance calls. If available, start with last year's totals for these items as a guide to estimating your future needs. Or use the amount from the expenditures you have recorded as a guide for your estimate.

The average family was defined by one person as "one that has an unexpected expense every month—but doesn't expect to have one this month!" How true it is! Maybe you should consider setting aside an amount for these "unexpecteds." Call it "Surprise."

This same worksheet can be used for as many as seven years. Use columns 1 and 2 for this year, 3 and 4 for next year, and so on. You will find it very interesting and easy to compare one year's plan to another year's.

When you have decided and recorded how much you choose to spend on each item of your money plan, add the figures and put the total on line 45. Staggering? Next, from your "estimate of Annual Income" work sheet, fill in the income section of your money plan.

Is the estimated income total on line 50 enough to cover what you have decided to spend? I hope so. If not, back to the drawing board. In column 2, you might want to record what percent each item is of the total. To calculate, divide the amount by the total on line 45. Such as:

Line 5, Housing $5,436
Line 45, Total $20,677
Housing percentage: $5,436 ÷ $20,677 = .2629 or 26.29 percent

These percentages can be helpful as you analyze your plan, in the light of what you want your priorities to be. These can also be compared with the sample percentages shown on the Expenditures Worksheet.

If your estimated annual income is not sufficient to cover your money plan, then your plan must be adjusted. Do not start your adventure into financial responsibility by adding to your debt. Remember, you cannot spend more than your income without facing rather harsh consequences somewhere down the line.

When your money plan for the year is complete, be sure to take the time to study it. Is it really you? Were you able to set aside savings for your dreams? Does it reflect your priorities? When the year is over, will you be in better shape than you are now?

Your "Money Plan" figures need to be divided by 12 and entered in column 1 on your "Expenditures Worksheet." (See example on following page.) This gives you a guideline to compare with each month's expenditures. I know you are going to enjoy recording your expenditures each month—it will be exciting to see how well you are doing or what areas you need to concentrate on, to do better. Sometimes I can hardly wait for the end of the month so that I can see how well we did in spending our money as we had planned.

Congratulations, you're on your way! Watch your financial situation improve! Enjoy the buoyant feeling that comes from knowing where you've been, where you are, and where you're going!

WILSON JONES

MONEY PLAN:

	1981 AMOUNT	%
Housing: Payment	$ 3816	
Utilities & Tel.	1380	
Maintenanc & Other	240	
Insur. & Taxes (Incl. on Line 1)	—	
TOTAL HOUSING	5436	26.29%
FOOD	3120	15.09%
TITHE	2600	12.57%
AUTO: GAS	1440	
Ins., Repairs, License	465	
TOTAL AUTO	1905	9.21%
INSURANCE: LIFE & MEDICAL	289	1.39%
DEBT PMTS: Credit Cards	216	
Installments	689	
AUTO	2071	
LOANS		
TOTAL DEBT PAYMENTS	2976	14.39%
CLOTHING	480	2.32%
"SURPRISE"	360	1.74%
SAVINGS	482	2.33%
MEDICAL EXPENSES (Incl. Grw. or FOR BRACES)	840	4.06%
ENTERTAINMENT & RECREATION		
Eating Out	520	
Vacations (Stay home this yr. See local attractions)	100	
Babysitters	150	
Other	72	
TOTAL ENTERTAINMENT & REC.	842	4.07%
OTHER: BEAUTY & BARBER SHOP	72	
Allowances	156	
Lunches	260	
Books, Subscriptions	-0-	
Gifts (Incl. Christmas)	500	
Music Lessons (piano)	360	
Education Expenses	-0-	
TOTAL OTHER	1348	6.53%
TOTAL EXPENDITURES	$ 20677	100%
INCOME: SALARIES, TAKE-HOME	$ 18127	
OTHER	2550	
TOTAL INCOME	$ 20677	

BILL'S
TV AND APPLIANCE
LIQUIDATION
SALE!
EVERYTHING MUST GO!!!
PRICED AT LEAST 20% LESS THAN THIS TIME NEXT YEAR!!

5

"She's Really Good at Spending Money"

"I don't know how I can do any better. I buy only the bare necessities as it is!"

Sound familiar? In many cases it may be true that we buy only necessities; but we probably could buy "better." "Almost any man knows how to earn money, but not one in a million knows how to spend it," wrote Henry David Thoreau.

I heard a man say, "My wife really knows how to spend our money." He didn't intend it as a compliment. But if, in fact, she is a good spender (good at getting her money's worth), then she should be complimented. Are you a good spender? Or only good at shelling out the cash and very poor at getting your money's worth? Do you buy wisely? Or do you buy impulsively, under pressure because "it's such a fantastic buy"?

Christmas spending is particularly hard on the family pocketbook. Elaborate gift giving has become a way of life. Many families do not finish paying off the debts incurred at Christmas until May of the following year. It is so easy to overspend, cajoled as we are by every retail store. We can charge and don't have to start paying until January; and we are given lists to mail to Santa Claus, complete with brand names and specifications.

I think the compulsion to buy gifts goes back to a feeling that we somehow have a duty to protect Santa's good image. Think of the price we pay! How in the world have we allowed ourselves to become saddled with the burden of this plump, jolly elf with the white beard?

The spiritual implication is staggering. We have attributed to Santa the ability to see all that goes on, to be everywhere at once, and to judge everyone. We are dangerously close to giving Santa the attributes of being omnipresent and omnipotent—attributes that rightly belong only to God. All sense and reason (and honesty) seem to leave us where Santa is concerned. If I had it to do over, I would not "train up my child" to love him, but rather to learn to adore the Babe "wrapped in swaddling clothes, lying in a manger."

The insidious result of falling into the Santa trap is that any semblance of order in budget planning is lost in the Christmas rush. Even for adults the feverish preparation and anticipation of gift-opening ends in letdown and disappointment. Children feel this same letdown and their disappointment (at not getting what they hoped for, or changing their minds after seeing someone else's gifts) is even more keen. Then comes the *BIG* depressive factor: the bills begin to arrive!

One fact of life is this: we will give gifts at Christmas. The question is, can we give them without causing financial disaster?

I have discovered a method of Christmas planning that has worked well for our family and has helped us keep our Christmas purchases within affordable limits. Early in the year I buy a small notebook, 4" x 6", that fits easily into my purse. (Don't make a special trip to the discount store to purchase one, however!) I label one page for every person we anticipate remembering with a gift. All during the year, when I see a need or hear someone express a "want," I write it down on that person's page. By August I am amazed to see the number of items I have listed, even for people who "have everything."

In September I get catalogs from three stores that I feel have competitive prices. As I go through them searching for the best price, I write the name of the store and their listed price in my book. Several months before Christmas we make our important decision: what will we spend for Christmas? With this dollar figure in mind, we go over our list of possible gifts and their prices to see which of the gifts we can afford. We have taken control of our Christmas spending (with the help of my little book), instead of our being swept along to a spending disaster.

Now the planning is over and the best part begins: the buying. I start searching advertised sales for the items in my book. Oh, the joy of bargain hunting! When I find an item for less than the best price in my book, I purchase it. This is exciting! I feel good about being able to buy gifts that are needed; I spend a lot less time in stores; and I know the prices I pay are the best available! There are very few items that I do not find on sale, and for those items I shop around for the best price. We have saved an average of 25 percent on all our expenditures. We've actually spent less than we had planned to spend! There is a great satisfaction in knowing you are in control of your spending.

But Christmas is not the only time of year we are caught up in overspending. One reason we rely so heavily on charge accounts during the holidays is that we have spent wildly preparing for school, for fall wardrobes, for new winter clothing, for spring outfits, and for vacation garb. Our bent for overspending knows no season. A casual jaunt through a shopping mall anytime can result in unplanned purchases. What was intended as a quick trip to the discount store to pick up a prescription or a notebook for Johnny can turn into month-end trauma as the basket is loaded with one small item after another (and a few large ones thrown in which happen to be on sale).

One important principle to remember in shopping is: Don't allow yourself to be sold. Salespersons, bless their hearts, can sometimes sell you on something you can't afford or don't need. Don't give up your initiative. You're the buyer. You decide for yourself.

Over a period of years I have accumulated ideas that might help you become a smarter shopper year-around. My ideas might help you avoid careless spending and help you get a dollar's worth of value for each dollar spent. They can help you shave dollars off of every area of your spending.

Food

Since this is a high-priority item, we will cover it first.

1. Plan your menus and make a shopping list. (Using your list at the store will save you time and help you avoid impulsive purchases of unnecessary items.)

2. Check for specials and stock up on such items you frequently use.

3. Buy produce only when it is in season and at a good price. (Freeze such items as chopped onions, parsley, and peppers.)

4. Buy day-old bread and pastries.

5. Don't shop when you are hungry.

6. Avoid convenience foods wherever possible; they cost more.

7. Compare prices, especially "unit prices" (how much an item costs per pound, per ounce, per pint, etc.).

8. Have milk delivered, if you use large quantities. It may be a few pennies more, but will save you going to the store so often. (I've never met a person who was able to go into a grocery store for one item and come out with only one item.)

9. Buy cases of items you use a lot. Check the phone

book Yellow Pages for wholesalers willing to sell to consumers.

10. Make your own frozen "TV" dinners with leftovers. (When my husband is out of town, I pull out the homemade frozen dinners and let the kids pick which they want.)

11. Freeze leftovers in "Seal-a-Meal" bags for future use.

12. Check for dates on containers to assure buying the freshest, especially in dairy products and other products requiring refrigeration. Also, to insure freshness, learn how to use the date color codes on bread and pastry products.

13. Try store brands or "private labels." If you are satisfied with the taste and quality, then buy them, for they are cheaper. (I like the canned fruit, tomato sauce, spaghetti sauce, and sandwich bags, to name a few, but I am not satisfied with the green beans, dish soap, or paper towels that come under the "private labels.")

14. Buy whole chickens and cut them up yourself.

15. Get a copy of *Your Money's Worth in Foods,* a free, 28-page booklet available from Consumer Information Center, Pueblo, CO 81009. To receive this helpful buyer's guide, send a postal card with your name and address and ask for Booklet No. 552F.

Housing

These expenses will probably be your largest expenditure each month, so should be considered carefully. There are advantages and disadvantages, other than financial considerations, in owning or in renting. These need to be considered as you decide whether to rent or buy.

Renting offers these advantages:

1. Flexibility. It is easier to move, which might be important if your job requires it.

2. Upkeep. The landlord normally makes repairs,

maintains the grounds, etc. This might be important to an elderly person or someone who travels a lot.

3. No down payment. You may not have the necessary cash for the down payment needed to buy. Or if you do, you can invest it in something else to yield income or appreciation or both.

Owning offers these advantages:

1. Pride and security in ownership.

2. Tax savings. Interest and property tax payments are deductible items for federal income taxes.

3. Appreciation. If inflation continues, you can expect your home to be worth more in later years.

4. Satisfaction in maintaining. Some people actually enjoy doing yard work and piddling around fixing up things.

For the financial considerations, follow through this example, as a guide to the kind of calculation you need to make in considering the facts as they apply to you.

To *rent* a two-bedroom apartment at $485 per month will cost $29,100 ($485 × 60 months), in five years. There are no tax savings and no appreciation of value. You will have received your shelter for five years and a pile of 60 rent receipts.

The same apartment unit is available for purchase as a condominium for $52,000. Assuming 10 percent down, a 30-year mortgage at 13⅞ percent, and a 30 percent income tax bracket; the costs will be:

	Money Expended for 5 Years
Down payment	$ 5,200
Monthly payments on $46,800 mortgage (including interest and insurance)	33,579
Condo maintenance fee, $95/month	5,700
Property taxes, $50/month	3,000
Electricity, $60/month	3,600
Repairs, $25/month	1,500
Total Money Expended	52,579

Less income tax savings from:	
Interest ($525 × 60 months × 30 percent)	(9,450)
Taxes ($50 × 60 months × 30 percent)	(900)
Buyer's out-of-pocket costs in five years	$42,229

These out-of-pocket costs amount to $617 per month, compared to $485 per month to rent. However, assuming a 10 percent rate of inflation and compounding the value increase, your $52,000 condo is now worth $83,000. If you sold it after five years, here's how the deal might look:

Sales price	$83,000
Less sales costs	6,000
	$77,000
Less mortgage balance	45,300
Amount you realize	$31,700

The difference between your out-of-pocket costs, $42,229, and the amount you realize from the sale, $31,700, is your cost for shelter for five years—$10,529. Compare this amount to the $29,100 cost to rent for the same period. Also consider that you will now have $31,000 cash from the sale due to your equity and the value appreciation.

Total housing costs should be held as close to the 30 percent of total income as possible. If mortgage payments of $617 per month are too high, the purchase of a smaller house may be indicated. With prices on homes rapidly escalating, along with interest rates, few young couples can afford these large payments and should beware of biting off more than they can chew. Using the same formula, one can compare buying with renting at a lower economic level to help determine which course is the best to take.

Utilities

It has been estimated that 30 percent of all energy used is wasted. About 54 percent of the energy used in homes goes into heating and cooling; about 15 percent is used to heat water; and the remainder is used for your range, refrigerator, and other appliances. With some imagination, I know that every one of us could cut down on the amount of energy we use. I've recently started washing clothes in cold water, insulated the water heater, and turned the temperature setting down. That's dollars saved.

Linens

1. Wait for "White Sales." These are usually in January and May, but can be at other times, so watch for advertising announcements.

2. Buy irregulars. Many times flaws are not even noticeable, but check the items carefully.

Clothes

1. Shop outlets.

2. Buy irregulars. Often flaws are inconspicuous, but still the article will be marked down as much as 50 percent.

3. Don't be afraid to call attention to a dirty or flawed item. Very often the store will reduce the price.

4. Give money at Christmas, then have a spending good time shopping on December 26, when clothing is marked down 30 percent to 50 percent.

Appliances

1. Don't buy appliances with additional gadgets you don't need.

2. Pick the brand and model you want, then use the phone to check the price at every store that carries it.

3. Sit tight till it's on sale.

Insurance

1. There *are* differences in price for the same coverage, so shop around.

2. Understand what is covered by your employer's medical insurance plan. You may be missing out on reimbursement for such things as prescriptions and dental bills.

3. Do not duplicate coverage already provided by an employer's or union's plan.

4. Term life insurance costs a fraction of what whole life or annuities cost. Learn the differences in coverage and choose the policy that meets your needs, as well as what you can afford.

5. Be aware that you can save a bunch by buying an automobile or homeowner's policy with a $250 or $500 deductible instead of the usual $50 or $100 deductible.

Some items provide seasonal savings. Plan ahead to take advantage of these seasonal bargains. The following "bargain calendar" was compiled using information from *Sylvia Porter's Money Book, Volume One.**

Bargain Calendar

January

Appliances
Bicycles
Linens
Clothes dryers
Furniture
Dishes and glassware
Shoes
Stereo equipment
Toys

February

Air conditioners
Bicycles
Clothes dryers
Furniture

---

*Sylvia Porter, *Sylvia Porter's Money Book, Volume One* (Garden City, N.Y.: Doubleday, 1975).

Stereo equipment
Toys

March

Clothes washers
Clothing (spring)
Ski equipment

April

Coats

May

Linens
Television sets

June

Television sets

July

Air conditioners
Bathing suits
Clothing (Summer)
Summer sports equipment

August

Air conditioners
Bathing suits
Camping equipment
Gardening equipment
Paint
New cars

September

Batteries and mufflers
Bicycles
Gardening equipment
Paint
New cars

October

Fishing equipment

November

Used cars
Lumber

December

Clothing (immediately after Christmas)
Used cars
Hunting equipment

I know you have many other ideas that will help you get your money's worth, so just use your own creative imagination.

Remember that to "shop smart" usually means to "shop around." This can be done through catalogues in your own home, or by using the phone, or by actually pounding the pavement.

Don't ever make a major purchase on an impulse. If you're tempted, STOP. Tell yourself and the salesperson, "I have to think about it, I have to shop around, and then maybe I'll buy."

Be *aware* of sales, but also *beware.* What glitters is not necessarily gold, so prepare yourself in advance to make an intelligent decision.

Let's face it, any woman worth her salt loves to shop and spend money. But shopping *smart* to get your money's worth can add a whole new, exciting dimension to shopping.

INTERNAL
REVENUE
SERVICE

6

Getting Our Act Together for the IRS

Oh, unhappy day—April 15!

Probably no chore is so despised, or performed under such contempt, as the preparation of our income tax returns. Normally efficient persons procrastinate. Methodical persons become disorganized. The psychological effect of the approaching deadline can be conservatively described as "devastating." And there seems to be no vicarious solace in the fact that everyone has to do it.

Mary Poppins sang,

> *Just a spoonful of sugar, helps the medicine go down, in a most delightful way.*

There is probably no "delightful" way to handle income taxes—but maybe there's an easier way. I suggest using a worksheet (the same paper we've used for our other schedules) to organize the information you need for preparing your tax return. I guarantee a worksheet such as this will take a great deal of the distress out of the traumatic 1040 by allowing you to get your information together—simply. Look at the format of the income tax worksheet on the following page.

Next, get out your last year's tax return and review it, before you put any headings on your own worksheet. This review will refresh your memory about the income items and deductible expenses you need to look for. Put headings on columns for the income (wages, interest, dividends, self-employment income, income from sales of assets, pensions, unemployment compensation, rental income, royalties, and others). Leave a blank column between each so that you can describe the source.

Now head up columns for deductible items. If you itemize your deductions on Schedule A of the 1040, head up the columns for the categories in the same order as they appear on Schedule A—medical insurance, medicine, doctors, dentists, hospital, and so on. You may need columns for items other than those on Schedule A; such as self-employment expenses, rental expenses, etc. Leave blank columns for descriptions, check numbers, dates, or whatever.

As I discussed in Chapter 2, accumulating information is much easier if you run everything through your checking account, both expenditures and receipts. If you have done this, most items on the worksheet can be picked up right out of your check register or off your check stubs.

Now, start with the first item you recorded in January in your check register or stubs. Examine each item carefully; and when you find an amount that applies to your tax return, write it down under the proper heading on the worksheet. In the blank column next to it, write the check number and date, and you might want to note to whom it was paid. Examine deposit entries also; and if an item represents taxable income, record it on your worksheet. When you finish going through your record of checks, you will have accumulated almost all the information you will need.

This task takes me approximately two hours each year. I do not pull out the cancelled checks or receipts to cover the items I have listed on the worksheet. They will only be needed to prove my figures in the unlikely event that we are audited by the Internal Revenue Service; so

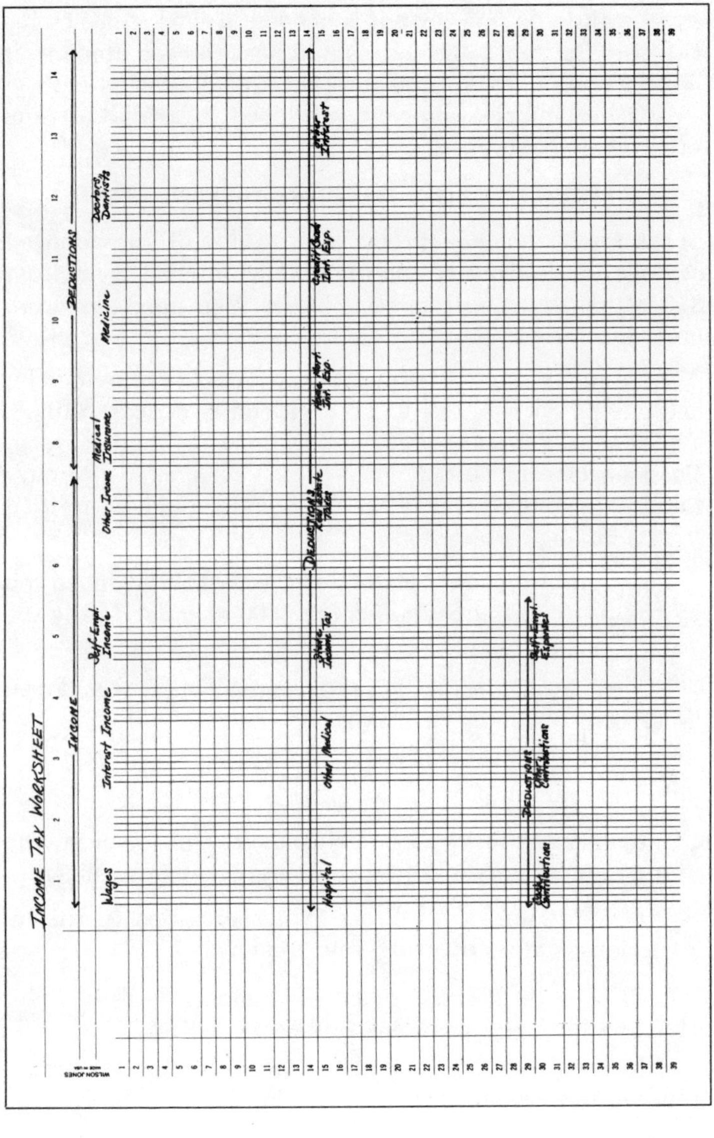
INCOME TAX WORKSHEET
INCOME
DEDUCTIONS
Wages
Interest Income
Self-Empl. Income
Other Income
Medical Insurance
Medicine
Doctors, Dentists
Hospital
Other Medical
State Income Tax
DEDUCTIONS
Real Estate Taxes
Home Mort. Int. Exp.
Credit Card Int. Exp.
Other Interest
Church Contributions
DEDUCTIONS
Other Contributions
Self-Empl. Expenses
WILSON JONES

I will wait to do this when it is needed, if ever. Since I have the check number and date noted next to each amount, it will be no big deal to find the cancelled checks later.

Other information you will need is available from other sources, such as:

Wages—From Form W-2 provided by employer.

Interest income—From Form 1099-INT provided by savings institutions if the amount of interest is at least $10.00. If less, it will be recorded in your passbook or on your quarterly savings statement.

Dividend income—From Form 1099-DIV provided by the paying corporation if the dividend is at least $10.00. Check this amount against your deposits for accuracy. Portions of some dividends are not considered ordinary taxable income. If this is the case, you should be notified by the paying corporation.

Royalties income—From Form 1099-MISC sent to you by the payor if the payments are $600 or more during the year.

Pension, annuities, or retirement pay—From Form W-2P sent to you by the payor.

State and local income taxes—From Form W-2 provided by your employer.

Real estate taxes—From statement sent to you by the mortgage company or found on your own expense sheet.

General sales tax—From tables provided in the instructions sent by IRS with your tax forms.

Interest expense, home mortgage—From statement sent to you by the mortgage company.

Interest expense, charge purchases—From statement sent by the credit card company or the retailer. Usually noted as "finance charges for the year" on the billing statement sent to you in January.

When you have entered every item on the worksheet, total each column. From here, it is a fairly simple matter to take these totals and enter them on the proper line on the 1040.

Using the "cookbook" method, attack your 1040 as though it were a recipe. Take one line at a time—read it and do what it says. Fill in the line if it applies to you, leave it blank if it doesn't, and go on to the next line. If you get stumped, follow the line-by-line instructions provided by the Internal Revenue Service with your tax forms. There is usually a section in these instructions covering changes in the law since the last year. It is a good idea to read through these "Highlights" before you write anything on the 1040, because they might save you some money. It is useless to try to explain each line item here because the format of the Form 1040 is changed somewhat each year. Believe it or not, these changes are usually to simplify the form. Read the instructions to determine if you are eligible to file Form 1040A. This is a shorter, simpler return to prepare.

After you fill in all applicable lines and you have recovered from the shock of seeing the "bottom line," check the entire return for errors; especially check math computations. I suggest you retain the original and make a copy to send to the IRS. If the mailing label from the forms booklet is correct, attach it to the space indicated on page 1. If you are filing a joint return, both husband and wife must sign it. Your Form 1040 is not considered a return unless it is signed. Now, don't forget to mail it before the deadline.

If the Internal Revenue Service determines there is a deficiency in the amount of income tax you paid, they can make an assessment for the additional tax. Generally, this assessment must be made within three years after your return is filed (the last day prescribed by law for filing if the return was filed before the last day). If, for example, you filed your return for 1978 on February 12, 1979, an assessment of deficiency could be made until April 15, 1982. Conversely, if you discover you have overpaid your income tax, you can file a refund claim any time within three years from the time your return was filed. There is no time limitation on assessment if a tax return is false or fraudulent or if no return is filed. Therefore, I suggest you keep copies of your returns and cancelled checks and other documents that support your income and deductions for at least three years three and one-half months after the year to which they apply. Example: Keep 1977 supporting documents until April 15, 1981; 1978 documents until April 15, 1982; and 1979 documents until April 15, 1983.

As you fill in your worksheet, if you think of different or better ways to accumulate information, make a note to yourself at the top or in the margin so you'll remember to do it the easier way next year. Now, put your copy of the completed tax return and your worksheet together in a file folder for easy reference next year at this time. I have 10 years of tax returns and worksheets in one folder, which makes it convenient if I need to refer to past years. All other supporting documents can be stored in a large manila envelope. Mark the outside "19—, income tax papers."

If someone else prepares your tax return, your completed worksheet will cut down on the preparation time. Tax practitioners usually charge by the hour, so less time for them means fewer charges for you. But remember you are still responsible for the accuracy of your return, so review it carefully before signing and mailing it.

Get busy and prepare your return right when you receive the forms you need—W-2s, 1099s, etc. These forms will normally be sent by January 31, and if you get right at it, you will probably spend less time at this task than the amount of time you will waste worrying about it as you procrastinate until April.

UNEMPLOYMENT
COMPENSATION

7

"Why Am I Still So Poor?"

John Whitney was the wealthy owner of four pawn shops. Those who borrowed on pawned items felt they were being cheated; and those who purchased forfeited items distrusted him. John had, in fact, taken advantage of many who were down on their luck and he had actually cheated others.

In spite of his wealth, John felt a gnawing emptiness in his life. He was not proud of the way he conducted his business, but never seriously considered changing. Finally, however, he allowed Jesus to fill the void in his life. He soon realized his wheeling and dealing was not pleasing to Christ. This conviction led him to give half of all he owned to needy families. Further, although this was very difficult for him to do, he tried to locate everyone he had cheated, admitted what he had done, and paid them back fourfold.

Jeremy Broadmore was the wealthiest man in his church. It was rumored that he had inherited in the neighborhood of $600,000 from his mother 15 years before. Through wise investments and business ventures, that inheritance had exploded into assets worth $2 million—give or take $100,000, depending upon what the financial markets were doing. He was a good, moral pillar of the community and loved and supported his church.

But his money and possessions meant more to him than anyone or anything else. The Holy Spirit convicted him of his need to change his attitude towards money and the priority it had in his life. For several years he struggled with this problem, but was not willing to change and finally gave up worrying about it. His wealth is increasing geometrically, but the pleasure of it is steadily decreasing.

Cal Rawls owned four sections—three of good grazing land and one of fertile bottomland. He had a bumper crop of barley and cotton. There was plenty of rain and mild weather, and his cattle thrived. However, the price for beef and grain was down. He decided to build storage facilities for his grain and hold off selling until the price went up. He delayed selling his heifers and steers, also. Six months later when the market improved, he made a huge profit on the sale of his grain and cattle which he plowed back into more land and cattle. He hired a ranch foreman and a farm manager and delegated the management of his property to them. Cal and his wife traveled extensively, but he lacked the refinement of a man who is used to moving in the higher strata of society and wealth; he was sometimes an embarrassment to his wife. Nevertheless, the Rawlses became known throughout the state for their showing off at extravagant parties. Two years ago, at age 38, Cal died of a massive heart attack, leaving a very rich widow.

People use their wealth in various ways and have different attitudes toward what they own. Stories similar to these three are recorded in Luke 19, Mark 10, and Luke 12. Wealth seems to be sought by nearly everyone, but it is a status fraught with risk. It takes a strongly committed Christian to remain spiritually upright under the weight of wealth.

Perhaps you're thinking: I wouldn't mind trying it for a while! You have scripture to back up that desire! God's Word has a load of promises for abundance in life—including financial abundance. (See the many scriptures listed in the appendix under "c.")

"If what you say is true," you may have asked yourself, "then why am I still so poor? Why can't I ever make ends meet?" I would like to say that these promises are for every believer, no ifs, ands or buts. But that's not exactly true. I believe that for many promises, there are conditions to be met—the ifs, ands or buts, if you will. Often *you* are required to do something before these promises can become operative, and you must be willing to do that "something." If a promise requires you to "pray," then you must pray. If it says "obey the Lord," then you must obey the Lord. If it says "give," then you must give. If it says "believe," then you must reach out your arms of faith. God is eager to fulfill His promises to us, but we must be willing to meet the conditions He has imposed. Otherwise our unwillingness can stand in the way of our receiving God's abundance.

There are other obstacles also that can block God's outpouring of blessings. The beautiful, tree-lined Abundance Boulevard is marred by potholes. The wise driver will steer clear of them. It is important to recognize and understand these pitfalls and to avoid them. In the following pages are listed some obstacles that I have recognized as blocking God's outpouring. I do not wish to hold these out as all-inclusive, but as common problems that I am familiar with.

Changing the Ends

"I can't seem to make ends meet!"

If you had $10,000 more income this year, would you still be moaning this familiar line? Possibly? or probably! We keep changing the *ends*. Sometimes we can't see it, but the truth is this: it wouldn't matter how much money we had because as revenues increase, needs (or what we think are needs) increase.

Visualize, if you please, a length of rope, two feet long, which represents your present income. You try to wrap it around a three-foot sphere which holds all your needs. Try as you might, you just will not be able to make those ends meet around the middle of the sphere. What you really need is a three-foot length of rope, right? Wrong! If your income increased to equal the three-foot length, what do you think would happen to the sphere full of needs? I'm afraid it would probably swell to the point that it would require a four-foot length to encircle it.

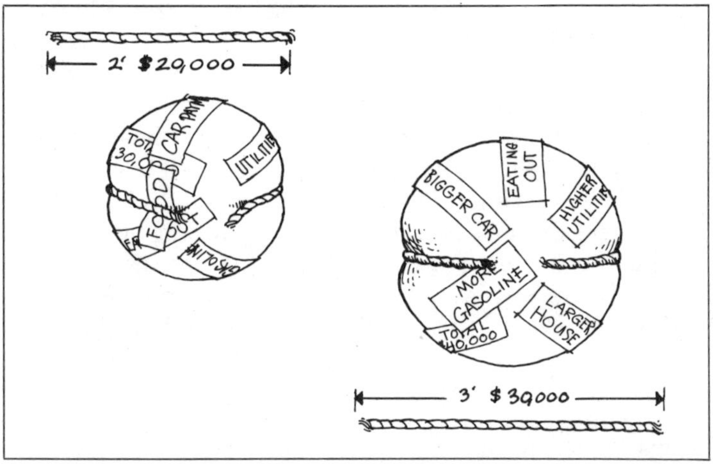

It has not occurred to many people that they need to reorganize expenditures to match their income, instead of always looking for ways to make more money. This very simple fact has somehow been hidden from our consciousness.

Let's take my friends, Jim and Elaine, who used to live down the street from me. They have three children, ages 5, 9, and 12. Jim is an accountant earning a substantial salary. A few years ago they received an unexpected windfall of $10,000—a testamentary bequest from Jim's

Aunt Sarah. They agreed that with this newfound wealth, they could afford the down payment on "that larger house we've needed for our growing family." They found the perfect place, were able to sell their present residence, qualified for the new loan, and moved in—all within three months. Their new home is situated in a more affluent neighborhood, and their neighbors welcomed them with food and assistance on moving day. It was an exciting event in their lives.

The children found many new friends in their new neighborhood. But—

Jim's children had been going to a $45.00/week Y.M.C.A. summer camp. Their new friends go to $300/week private camps in Colorado.

Their new friends have 10-speeds, go-carts, mopeds, and dirt bikes. Jim's children don't have any of these things.

The adult neighbors belong to the country clubs, play golf and tennis, and drive new luxury cars.

Pressure first started to come from the children to have the things their friends have. Then Jim and Elaine began to rationalize that they too "needed" the toys their adult friends enjoyed, even though their income was not sufficient to support this new life-style.

To "make ends meet," Elaine got a job. She hired a live-in maid to do the housework and care for the children after school. In addition to the salary for the maid, there was the increased cost of cleaning supplies, food, gasoline, clothing, and taxes. Elaine was naturally tired at the end of each day, so she and Jim had occasional arguments, usually preceded by discussions about their money problems. These arguments became more frequent; in fact, they became a wedge dividing the family.

Finally two years after their move, Jim and Elaine woke up to what was happening: Instead of really living, they were trying to pursue a life-style, and they were miserable! This realization was their first and most important positive step in getting their act back together. They sold their home and moved back to their old neighborhood. They set aside $2,000 in a certificate of deposit for emergencies and $6,000 for a college fund for the kids. They paid off their debts and Elaine quit her job. She is back to taking care of her own household.

Their $10,000 windfall eventually caused them headaches and heartaches. They couldn't make ends meet, because they changed the ends.

Discontent

What kind of message are we sending to God?

The fact that we are willing to go into debt in order to acquire things or services immediately—before we have earned the money to pay for them—must indicate to God we are not content with what we have. Our insatiable appetite for things is whetted by easy access to the little plastic credit cards. Our abundance of possessions or lack of them is not the problem! Our problem is the paramount importance we place on possessions, and our discontent and even greed when we don't have them. Credit buying is merely a symptom of this problem of discontent.

God will give you the ability to be content with what you have and the wisdom to help you get your money priorities straight. The next time you are tempted to purchase something you really can't afford, stand on this promise in Hebrews 13:

> *Keep your lives free from the love of money and be content with what you have, because God has said,*
>
> *"Never will I leave you;*
> *never will I forsake you"* (verse 5).

What more can we ask for than that?

Irresponsible Managers

Jesus often used parables to teach the multitudes that crowded around Him. Once He told His followers of a master who left three servants in charge of various amounts of valuables while he was away on a journey. When he returned, he required an accounting from the servants and discovered that two had used these valuables wisely. To each of these, the master exclaimed:

> *Well done, good and faithful servant! You have been faithful with a few things; I will put you in charge of many things. Come and share your master's happiness!* (Matt. 25:23).

What a lesson for us! How can we expect God to entrust us with more than we already have, if we have not proved to Him that we can use wisely the resources we now control. Wise use includes knowing what our resources are and then carefully using them. This knowledge requires, among other things, record keeping and planning ahead.

In the parable above, the servant who did not do an adequate job had his resources taken away from him.

Talking Too Much

I will take the liberty to paraphrase what Jesus had to say about giving. "When you give, shhhhhhhhhh." Perhaps that is too simply put, but in essence that's what He said in the scripture passage from Matthew 6:

> *When you give to the needy, do not announce it with trumpets, as the hypocrites do in the synagogues and on the streets, to be honored by men. I tell you the truth, they have received their reward in full. But when you give to the needy, do not let your left hand know what your right hand is doing, so that your giving may be in*

secret. Then your Father, who sees what is done in secret, will reward you (verses 2-4).

I am grieved each time I hear people making the righteous point that "they tithe," or that "they give such and such." These persons may in fact receive the respect and honor of men, but their blabbing blocks the abundant blessings God has for them.

Keep your giving a secret—between you and God—and don't be guilty of talking too much.

Disbelief

Perhaps we don't really believe that God will do what He says He will do. If we do not believe that God really is trustworthy to do what He says, then those promises are "of no value" to us.

Sometimes our actions reveal our disbelief. Ulcers, nervous insomnia, high blood pressure, and stomach disorders, among other physical symptoms, testify to the fact that we *are* anxious about tomorrow. And this negative confession of our lack of faith in God's trustworthiness makes His promises "of no value" to us. In other words, the promises won't work for us if we don't believe them.

Cursing Taxes

Can we curse income taxes without cursing the God-given income on which those taxes are computed? By our utterance condemning taxes are we petitioning God for less taxes? If so, an immediate answer to this petition might be less income!

Theft

One of the Ten Commandments is "You shall not steal" (Exod. 20:15).

There are more subtle ways to steal than to burglarize a home or embezzle money. Pilferage, misrepresentation, wasting time, and evasion of taxes, to name a few, can all be stealing. But stealing by any other name is still stealing, and these dishonest acts can block our receiving the abundant prosperity God wishes us to have. Therefore it is extremely important to be aware of these things that displease God.

> *The Lord your God detests anyone who does these things, anyone who deals dishonestly* (Deut. 25:16).

As employees

In Luke 16, Jesus tells of an employee who wastes his employer's assets. He was fired, but thought of a scheme to insure that he would not go hungry. The fired man called in his employer's debtors and he forgave the indebtedness of some of their accounts, in return for the promise of future favors for himself. His employer commended him for his shrewdness, but went on to say:

> *Whoever can be trusted with very little can also be trusted with much, and whoever is dishonest with very little will also be dishonest with much. So if you have not been trustworthy in handling worldly wealth, who will trust you with true riches? And if you have not been trustworthy with someone else's property, who will give you property of your own?* (verses 10-12).

The losses from employee pilferage are enormous. These thefts, it is estimated, cost employers $50 billion in 1980. As mind-boggling as that figure is, the cost to the dishonest employee is even greater. Think what he is losing out on. Every pencil, paper clip, ruler, or file folder carried home by an employee costs him dearly, because these *little* things are just as important to a righteous God, as the things on which the world places greater value. Stealing a paper clip is just as sinful as embezzling thousands of dollars.

Employee expense accounts are an area notorious for cheating. But just because "everyone else" is milking those expense allowances, does not excuse this dishonesty by a Christian.

Have you heard these justifications for stealing?

"Management is so wasteful; they will never miss this!"

"I deserve this!"

"This will help to make up for the fact that I'm underpaid!"

Look again at Luke 16:12,

> *If you have not been trustworthy with someone else's property, who will give you property of your own?*

An employee's *time* certainly is part of the employer's property. But a recent University of Michigan report states that employees spend 8 to 11 percent of their time at work, not working.

I was recently waiting in a business office for an appointment and observed two young men employees sitting at adjoining desks. They were enthusiastically discussing the evening college courses they were attending. Once they stopped talking long enough for one of them to punch several numbers into his calculator, shuffle some papers around, and write something on a worksheet. Then they resumed their conversation and discussed the courses they were interested in attending next semester. This conversation was still going on when I was called in for my appointment—20 minutes later.

Employees waste their employer's time in many ways —making personal phone calls, taking long coffee breaks, conducting personal business while on the job. Often the rationale may be, "I'm not getting paid what I'm worth, so why should I give my best effort." This rationale sounds reasonable, but it ignores the fact that when a person accepts a job, he accepts the terms of employment, including compensation. Therefore, you *owe* your employer your best effort.

As employers

James tells about employers who cheated some of their employees out of their wages. In chapter 5 of his letter, he describes very vividly what will become of them:

> *Now listen, you rich people, weep and wail because of the misery that is coming upon you. Your wealth has rotted, and moths have eaten your clothes. Your gold and silver are corroded. Their corrosion will testify against you and eat your flesh like fire* (Jas. 5:1-3).

That's pretty heavy stuff.

Business persons must guard against dishonesty in all areas of their business dealings, not just in dealing with employees. Customers, suppliers, and clients all deserve honesty. In advertising and other communication to the general public, Christians must be truthful and reliable.

I have heard that "it just isn't possible" to survive in the secular world of business if we try to carry on in a manner pleasing to God. But I hold strongly that just the opposite is true: "If God is for us, who can be against us?" (Rom. 8:31*b*). With God on our side, how can we lose? "The people of this world are more shrewd in dealing with their own kind than are the people of light" (Luke 16:8*b*), but with God as our Chairman of the Board, we are lifted to the level of fair competition. The success stories of many Christian business men and women testify to this. God honors those who honor Him!

Trying to straddle the fence of righteousness, being a Christian on weekends but acting like a heathen on the job, won't work. Leaving God at home when we go to the office can bring disaster.

As taxpayers

Cheating on income taxes is stealing! God expects of us honesty in all things, and taxes are no exception. Do you believe that? Evidently many people do not! Many brag openly of how they cheat on their income tax returns.

During the time Jesus lived on earth, a Temple tax was levied on the Israelites. This tax was resented, but Jesus didn't try to cheat or avoid paying it. When the collectors came to Peter and asked if Jesus would pay the tax, Jesus provided the money to pay the tax for himself and Peter. Read Matthew 17 to see the interesting way God provided for this necessity.

As a certified public accountant, I realize there are many ways to evade paying taxes, and some of these schemes would be very difficult to detect by investigators. But regardless of how unlikely is the possibility of being caught, fraudulent evasion of taxes is illegal and can subject the liable person to civil penalties and/or criminal penalties.

God expects more of us than that!

As givers

> *A tithe of everything from the land, whether grain from the soil or fruit from the trees, belongs to the Lord, it is holy to the Lord* (Lev. 27:30).

The tithe is ten percent of what we produce or earn.

> *Will a man rob God? Yet you rob me.*
> *But you ask, "How do we rob you?"*
> *In tithes and offerings* (Mal. 3:8).

Need I say more?

As consumers

Accepting excessive change at the check-out ("It's the cashier's error, so let him pay for it"); switching price tags ("They charge too much anyway"); shoplifting ("They make enough profit to cover it"). Most consumer dishonesty wouldn't happen if someone were looking. Well, God is looking! And the punishment we bring on ourselves, from God, for these petty larcenies should frighten all of us.

Being less than completely honest in all our affairs can really knock a hole in our pail of prosperity. And a leaky pail is not what God desires for us.

Devout people, through no fault of their own, sometimes suffer severe financial reverses and occasionally suffer great physical need. God's purposes in such cases are unknown to us. Sometimes, as with Job, such adverse situations are temporary; at other times, as in undeveloped and Communist-ruled countries, poverty is a way of life for most people, with Christians being singled out for more suffering than others, simply because of their faith. While acknowledging these situations (to which the Early Church certainly could relate), I believe that God wants us to be happy; He wants to meet our needs. God wants us to be winners!

For some people, prosperity in the form of financial wealth may not be a good thing. Some people simply cannot handle wealth. As you increase your money management skills and are able to deal with finances in the responsible way God intended, He will entrust you with more good things.

I believe God wants us to have abundant prosperity. He promises it. And He has the assets to back up His promises! We have a wealthy Father indeed, and He takes pleasure in our prosperity. Webster defines *prosperity:* "The condition of being successful or thriving; *esp:* economic well-being."

"The Lord be magnified, Who delights in the prosperity of His servant" (Ps. 35:27, NASB). All the resources in the world are at God's disposal. He either has made all things or has given us the ability to make them. "The earth is the Lord's, and everything in it" (1 Cor. 10:26); "But remember the Lord your God, for it is he who gives you the ability to produce wealth" (Deut. 8:18*a*).

A part of God's plan is that we have to be dependent upon some worldly things—such as money. But God has allowed us the authority to rule and subdue. We are not to be under subjection to anything or anyone, except God. He wants us to do more than just cope with money. He wants us in control, and He gives us the ability to handle and manage our affairs and finances in such a way that money should not be the oppressing burden or depressing dilemma that it has become for some people.

God's promises are for *you.* (These promises, some of them, are listed in the Appendix.) "All these blessings will come upon you and accompany you if you obey the Lord your God" (Deut. 28:2). These blessings are enumerated throughout that chapter and include the following blessings from Deut. 28:11-12:

> *The Lord will grant you abundant prosperity—in the fruit of your womb, the young of your livestock and the crops of your ground—in the land he swore to your forefathers to give you. The Lord will open the heavens, the storehouse of his bounty, to send rain on your land in season and to bless all the work of your hands. You will lend to many nations but will borrow from none.*

To the person who delights in God's law comes the promise:

> *Whatever he does prospers* (Ps. 1:3*b*). *For the Lord God is a sun and shield; the Lord bestows favor and honor; no good thing does he withhold from those whose walk is blameless* (Ps. 84:11).

Then why am I so poor? The wonder is that God has

entrusted me with as much as He has! As I recognize and understand these obstacles to God's promised prosperity, the potholes on Abundance Boulevard, I am better able to steer clear of them. I realize now that if I'm not living in abundance, it's probably my fault, not God's.

Overriding all that God wants for me is His wish that I have what is best for me. If I cannot demonstrate the ability to manage, handle, and properly use money, then it is probably not in my best interests to have an abundance of it. And whether I believe it or not, God knows better than I do what is best for me!

WHILE THEY LAST
SALE

8

Credit: Privilege or Curse?

For 3,000 years money has been used as a medium of exchange and until just 50 years ago money management was fairly easy. A person with cash could buy and a person without cash couldn't buy. But in just the last half century, consumer credit has been available on a large scale, which has made life and money management considerably more complicated.

Credit is a privilege—the privilege of using goods or services before you pay for them. But the other side of the credit coin is debt. And for the overextended debtor—credit can be more a curse than a privilege.

Here are some interesting statistics:

- In August, 1980, the people of the United States owed $303.4 billion on credit cards, car loans, and personal loans. (That is an average of $1,350 for every person.)
- In January, 1979, Americans owed $1 trillion on their homes.
- In 1978, we added $45 billion more to our debts than we paid off.
- One-half of the sales of large retail department stores come through charge cards.

Americans' penchant for buy-now-pay-later fairly staggers the imagination. The *average* family is having to use almost 20 cents out of every take-home dollar to repay consumer debt—and that does not include the home mortgage debt. But one-fifth of all households owe no debt at all, so the amount of income going to debt service (by those who owe money) is closer to 33 cents of every dollar. And there are a significant number of families that must allocate almost 50 cents of every dollar for debt service!

In the spring of 1980, the Federal Reserve Board imposed consumer-credit controls. This unusual bit of regulation is credited for the fact that in April and May of that year, consumer installment debt fell for the first time in recent history. For those two months, consumers actually paid back more than they added to their debts. But in July, 1980, the Federal Reserve Board dismantled the controls it had imposed just four short months before. The headlines on July 9 heralded—"It's business as usual for credit card customers." But those two months showed Americans could live with less credit. Too bad it took a regulatory agency to make us realize this.

All these statistics and regulations are just a lot of hoopla unless and until they involve you and me personally. How are you personally affected by credit and debt?

Every person I know has at some time used consumer credit, defined as "credit used by individuals and families for personal needs." Responsibly used credit has many benefits, some of which are:

1. The convenience of not having to carry large amounts of cash.
2. The convenience of receiving one bill each month, usually with a record of purchases.
3. Being able to take advantage of sales prices when out of cash.
4. Being able to purchase and begin using an item immediately.

The fact that the United States has had almost continuous inflation during the last 40 years must also be considered in our discussion of the benefits of consumer credit.

Charles A. Luckett, a consumer debt expert at the Federal Reserve Board, in an interview for a newspaper, observed that "Adopting a strategy of not owing anything to anybody may not be very realistic in an inflated economy. It might make more sense to borrow now and pay back later in cheaper dollars." This idea of the desirability of being in debt in a time of inflation is expounded from every direction. But I strongly believe and cannot emphasize enough: *Consumer debt is not a hedge against inflation!* Remember that consumer debt is debt incurred for personal needs. It is unwise and self-defeating to use this kind of debt as a means of beating inflation. It is true that incurring debt to make sound *long-term* investments may be wise provided monthly payments are in line with earnings capability. But here we are limiting our discussion to consumer debt for personal needs—not investments.

Let's consider Mark and Monica's financial plight. They had used their credit to the limit to buy such items as a car, a dishwasher, clothes dryer, furniture, golf clubs, and clothing because due to inflation they reasoned, "these items will cost more later if we wait." Mark and Monica relied on both of their incomes to make regular payments on these debts and managed very well.

In 1980 we did have double-digit inflation, but we also had a period of economic slowdown accompanied by increased unemployment. Monica was unexpectedly laid off during this economic slump and with only Mark's income, they found it impossible to keep up their debt payments. Some of their household goods were repossessed and they were harassed by creditors to the point they saw no alternative but to file a petition of bankruptcy. Sadly, their plight is not an isolated incident. This is but one example of the disaster that can await those who are in debt to the hilt on the mistaken assumption this is a wise course in view of continued inflation.

Almost every day, then, the decision must be made—"Do I buy now on credit, or do I wait until I can pay cash?" Let's consider two different purchases, figure the actual cash outlay (actual cash out-of-your-pocket), and study what options might be available to you.

First, let's look at the purchase of a piano. You can buy a nice, but inexpensive console today for $1,299. The music company will accept $133.95 down and you can take 36 months to pay it out at $48.61 per month. That's not bad. Right? Well, maybe! Let's take a closer look.

At the end of 36 months, you will have an actual cash outlay of $1,883.91 [$133.95 + (36 × $48.61)]. But if you plan ahead for this piano purchase or feel as if you can put off buying and start a savings account with the proposed payments, here's what can happen: You use the $133.95 to open a savings account paying 5.5 percent interest and each month thereafter you deposit the equivalent of the monthly payment, or $48.61. In *two* years' time you would have more than enough to buy the piano.

Your actual cash outlay ($133.95 plus 23 deposits of $48.61)	$1,251.98
Interest earned	73.07
Total available at the time of the final monthly deposit	$1,325.05
Actual cost of piano	$1,299.00

At this writing, you might choose, instead, to save until you have accumulated $500, which can then be put into a money market fund earning 14 percent. At that rate, you would have the purchase price in just 21 months. Your cash outlay would be $1,154.76, and you would have earned almost twice the interest: $144.46.

To recap, at today's rate, if you acquire the piano immediately and pay over 36 months, your actual cash outlay will be	$1,883.91

But if you wait and save for 21 months, your actual cash outlay will be	1,154.76
Therefore, the additional cost to buy now is	$ 729.15

That's 63 percent more!

Consider these points in your decision to buy now or later:

1. If you have visions of your child being a great pianist, check with a teacher as to what age he should start playing, and start saving. Instrument payments that have to be made at the same time as the payment for lessons, music, transportation, music contests, and a metronome can put a kink in anyone's money plan.

2. If the right age and an eager child (is there such?) are upon you and you haven't already stashed away enough for the instrument, consider renting. You can rent for six months, and then if you decide to buy, the rental payments can usually be applied to your purchase. Remember, many children are just not going to enjoy or be interested in music and usually you will know within a few months if it will be worthwhile to continue. You could end up stuck with a $1,300 piece of useless furniture, a child with no interest (and maybe even no talent), and 30 or more monthly payments of almost $50.00.

3. Check the want ads for unfortunates who got stuck with a barely used, practically new piano, and are willing to get rid of it for a real bargain price.

4. If inflation continues, what will the piano cost in two years? You would naturally assume it will be more, but during the last two years, when inflation rates have been about 10 percent per year, the price of this less expensive piano has not increased.

Next, let's look at the purchase of an automobile. But first let's tear down some assumptions that have become ingrained in the thinking of many.

1. Don't assume you must have a *new* car. I have been driving for 23 years and have never had a new car. I also have not had any more problems or repair bills than those I know who always purchase new cars. I must qualify that statement. For the past year I have had more than usual repair expenses on my five-year-old faithful Ford. But I can trace this rash of repairs back to the time I let her radiator run dry, and continued to drive her until she began to knock and smoke started to pour out from underneath. At that point I was forced to abandon her beside the road. She has not forgiven me this indignity, and I'm paying through the nose for her problems.

Second. Don't assume you must *always* live with car payments. There may be another way.

To purchase and finance a $6,500 automobile, our banker says you will have to pay $1,300 down, and the remaining $5,200 at $152.70 for 48 months. After 48 months you will have an actual cash outlay of $7,329.60 ($152.70 × 48) assuming the trade-in value of your old vehicle equals the required down payment. But if you continue to drive your old vehicle and deposit $152.70 each month in a certificate or fund earning 14 percent (this could fluctuate), here's what will happen:

You have an actual cash outlay in 29 months of	$4,428.30
You have earned interest of	780.59
You have the purchase price in 29 months	$5,208.89

This assumes you can still use your old car as the down payment.

To recap, if you acquire the car immediately and pay over 48 months, your actual cash outlay will be	$7,329.60
If you wait and save for 29 months at the higher rate, your actual cash outlay will be	4,428.30

Therefore, the additional cost to buy now on credit is $2,901.30

That's 65 percent more!

But also consider these points in your decision to buy now or later:

1. Will your old car last another 29 months?
2. Will the price of a new car be greater in 29 months? If so, how much?
3. Will you be better off to shop for a used car?

In this discussion of the piano and the automobile, we ignored one factor that should be considered in arriving at the actual cash outlay—income taxes. If you take the standard deduction on your tax return, the finance charges you pay will have no effect. However, if you itemize your deductions, then finance charges will reduce your taxable income and therefore your tax. Also interest earned on your savings will increase your taxable income with a resultant income tax increase.

"To have or not to have—NOW?" that is the question. As you face these decisions every day, ask yourself these questions:

1. Do I really need it?
2. Do I really need it, *now?*
3. Can I rent it?
4. Will I still be using it two years from now?
5. Will it cost more later?
6. What is the actual cash outlay if I buy now and pay later?
7. What is the actual cash outlay if I save now and buy later?
8. Can I afford it now? Or later? Or ever?

Talk over these questions with some knowledgeable person, because verbalizing can help you get your ideas in perspective, generate new ideas, and let you see the choices more clearly.

There are distinct differences and, therefore, distinct choices for you to make in deciding to use cash or to buy on credit. And the choices are yours. Don't let some enthusiastic salesperson stampede you into a decision that you might regret later. Remember too, *if you cannot afford to save for a purchase, you cannot afford the payments on a credit purchase anyway.*

Consumer credit and the resulting debt burden on you and me are here to stay. Is it a privilege or a curse? It has the potential to be either—depending upon how we handle it. "Credit is a privilege—don't abuse it!" states the credit bureau advertisement. Misuse and abuse of credit can result in a debt burden heavier than you'll be able to bear. A pile of unpaid bills can lead to frustration and stress that no family needs.

Do you have too many bills? Are you overextended? There are warning signs that may indicate you are approaching the debt-danger zone, where credit becomes a curse rather than a privilege. Do these warning signs apply to you?

1. More than 20 percent of your take-home pay goes to make debt payments.
2. You have little or no savings to meet emergencies.
3. You depend upon extra income to make it: moonlighting, bonuses, etc.
4. You pay the minimum amount on revolving accounts, and the new charges exceed the payment you made.
5. You receive "second notices" and letters regarding overdue payments.
6. You have to charge necessities: groceries, clothing, etc.
7. You are considering a consolidation loan.

Are you approaching the danger zone? Figures indicate many people have already arrived! In the next chapter, we'll discuss exercises to get out-of-shape financial situations back into shape.

Should a Christian allow himself to get into debt? I have heard such responses as:

"Debt is always sinful!"

"Debt is usually okay for Christians, as long as they keep up their payments."

"All debt is sinful except for home mortgages."

What do you think? The answer for me might not necessarily be the answer for you. "Circumstances alter cases" is a correct maxim. Credit can help a person over a financial "hump," and without a home mortgage most families could never buy a home. When credit is used as a standby for emergencies a yellow caution light goes on, and one must be very careful not to allow credit to become a continuing crutch. The best solution, of course, is to seek God's will through prayer in every credit decision you make and to be sensitive to the nudging of the Holy Spirit. This rules out impulsive credit purchases, the worst culprit. If such purchases have been shattering your best-laid money plans, perhaps you need to be ready with "Get thee behind me, Satan," when you're tempted to buy.

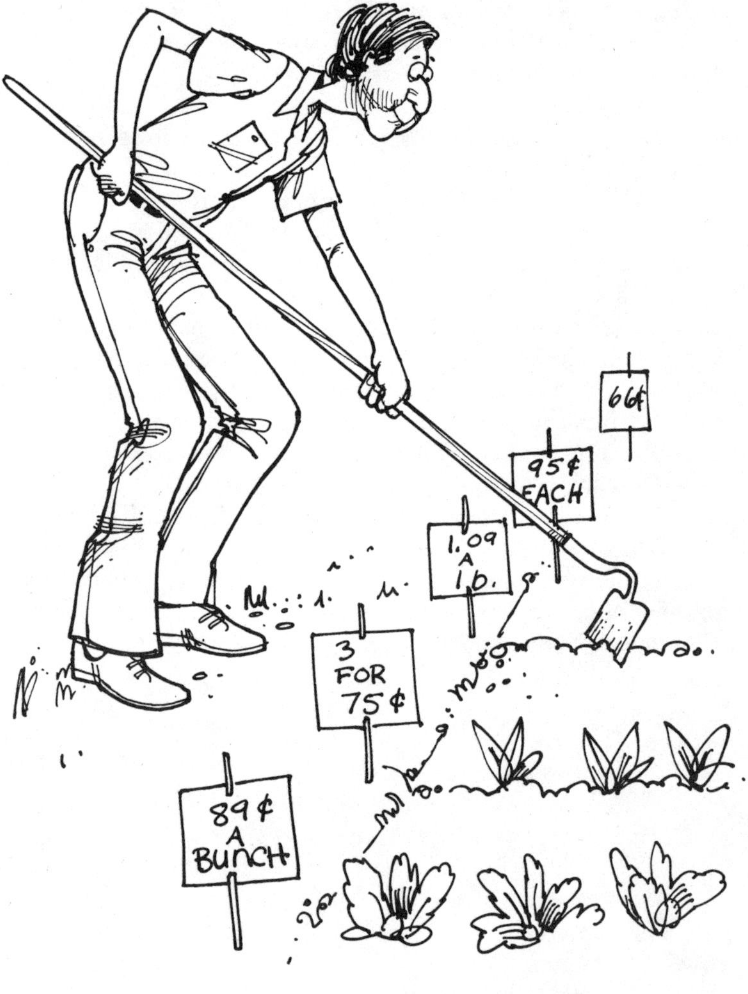
66¢
95¢
EACH
1.09
A
lb.
3
FOR
75¢
89¢
A
BUNCH

9

Financial Dieting

If you're an overextended debtor—*you know it!* You lose sleep worrying about your debts. You panic when you sit down to pay bills. Depressed, you wonder if there's a light at the end of the tunnel. Or even an end to the tunnel.

Knowing you have a problem is the first step towards solving it. We tend to worry more about monsters lurking in dark corners than about skeletons hanging out in the open. So let's get that skeleton of unpaid and maybe past due bills out of the closet and into the light so we can deal with it.

Start by making a worksheet listing all of your unpaid bills. (A simple schedule is illustrated on the next page.) It is important that you list complete information. If you are not sure of remaining balances or terms of payout, call your creditor and ask. Your worksheet should reflect only those debts that you intend to pay out over a period of more than one month. Seeing your debt information in black and white will be invaluable as you plan a solution. It is important, too, to level with everyone in your family; explain the situation to them, and you'll be amazed at their eagerness to cooperate.

The villain in your financial melodrama could be unexpected medical bills or unemployment or a death in the family or a natural disaster. But more likely the culprits were your desires for more and more "things," the availability of almost unlimited credit, and inflation.

UNPAID BILLS:

OWING TO	DATE INCURRED	TOTAL AMT. OWING YOU	MONTHLY PMT. REQUIRED	DATE TO BE PAID OFF	FINANCE CHARGES
AT 12/15/79					
Sears (sewing machine)	6/79	# 175.00	# 30.00	6/80	18%
Dept. Store (revolving chgs.)	various	549.00	25.00	10/81	18%
VISA (furniture)	12/79	836.00	40.00	9/81	18% on #500, 12% on rest
Bank (car)	3/79	4660.47	172.61	3/82	11.96%
		# 6220.47	# 267.61		
AT 11/30/80					
Dept. Store (revolving chgs)	various	# 389.00	# 25.00	3/82	18%
VISA (furniture)	12/79	356.00	18.00	9/82	18%
Bank (car)	3/79	2589.15	172.61	3/82	11.96%
Dr. Stevens	9/80	389.00	50.00	8/81	-0-
		# 3723.15	# 265.61		

Desires for More and More "Things"

As has already been mentioned, one culprit is the undue importance we place on possessions. We desire more and more "things" and as a result we have become a nation of spoiled kids who expect to get everything we want, *right now*. An incident I observed last week helps to illustrate this.

I was waiting in line to check out at the grocery store and became fascinated with the three-year-old boy sitting in the cart in front of me. He was making a shambles of the candy and gum in the rack right beside him. He was trying to tear open a package of gum with his teeth when his mother realized what he was doing, took the gum away and put it back in the rack. At this, the kid let out a squall that attracted everyone's attention. His mother went back to sorting her purchases, and he went for a candy bar. He drooled on it, she grabbed it and put it back in the rack, which made him scream even louder. By now everyone was wondering with curiosity who was going to win this little war.

The lady's purchases were almost checked through and the kid was attacking another package of gum. He let out such an ear-shattering squeal this time that no doubt even the customers back in the produce department heard him. At this his mother lamely said, "Well, all right, but you can have just one piece." I shook my head and thought of what I could accomplish in just 30 seconds with that spoiled child.

Now, there is some spoiled brat in each of us—some more than others. Sometimes we just must slap our own hand and say, "No, no!!" We must grow up and accept the fact that we can't have everything we see and want. That is discipline, and it suggests maturity.

Almost Unlimited Credit

The availability of almost unlimited credit has encouraged our buy-now, pay-later shopping habits. Often charge accounts are opened by retail stores and charge cards are issued by banks with very little consideration given to the ability of a person to pay off these potential credit limits. There's a growing number of "chargaholics" and "credit card junkies." Your little plastic cards can delude you into thinking you're on Easy Street when in fact you're coasting toward calamity. In the past, consumers often became bogged down in a financial mire by borrowing to improve their life-styles, to surround themselves with luxuries. They insisted on pleasures today at the expense of tomorrow. For them, yesterday's tomorrow is here today. Those same families now are using credit to buy *necessities.*

Inflation

This is one culprit over which you have no control. However, proper planning can help ease the burden of inflation. If you are convinced this upward direction in prices will continue, it is important to build adequate amounts into your money plan to cover the expected increased cost of living in the future. Don't just wring your hands in despair. Face this culprit and plan ahead. This might mean cutting down or cutting out entirely some items in your money plan in order to be able to afford the increased cost of other items.

But regardless of which is the star villain in your financial melodrama, the resulting fact is: *You're in trouble.* The important thing now is to do something about it.

Fat! What do you think when you hear that word? Most persons in the United States immediately think of "me." We are a nation of overweight people, and we have literally become a nation of experts on dieting. If reading, studying, and talking about a subject can result in expertise, then almost every woman I know qualifies as a Certified Professional Dieter. Dieting, simply put, is "doing without." Whatever the diet, the principle is the same, "doing without"—calories, or carbohydrates, or everything but grapefruit, or whatever.

So what does this have to do with your debt problem? Just this. My proposed solution to your debt obesity is *financial dieting.* The principle is the same as in food dieting—"doing without." Generally, financial dieting needs only to be practiced for a limited time, the length of time being determined by the shape you are in when you start. Although you may have gotten out-of-shape because of circumstances beyond your control, more than likely it was due to your own overconsumption.

Here's how your financial diet can work. If you are. in

fact, not able to make your debt payments on time or are already past due, work out what you feel you can pay on each account. Record these amounts in a column on your unpaid bills schedule. Plan to start your diet on a special day. On that first day call each of your creditors. Explain your problem, outline how you will be able to pay out the account, and ask for their approval. Let them know if you are proposing a pay-out over a longer period of time than was originally agreed upon. Every credit manager and collector I know will appreciate the fact that you are trying, and will probably be glad to assist you. Now collect all your credit cards. Either destroy them or hide them away and resolve not to use them. Abstain from buying with credit entirely.

Next decide what you are willing to do without. Start by cancelling out every single thing except absolute necessities. Consider your new life-style during this diet as one of "voluntary simplicity." Try it for just one month. During that month write down what you wanted to buy but didn't. Also how much those things would have cost. After the first month review the list of things you refused to buy. Such a list might look like this:

Beauty shop, 4 times	$30.00
Eating out, 6 times	85.00
Toaster	16.00
Skirt and sweater	33.00
Tennis racket	14.50
Cassettes, 2	13.00
	$191.50

It's amazing how much this "voluntary simplicity" life-style can save. Use the money you didn't spend to pay off some of those unpaid bills. Try another month of the same—just the bare necessities. Can you see the unsightly bulges on your unpaid bills schedule start to melt away? How long this rigorous abstinence should last depends entirely upon how much you want to lose and how quickly. Perhaps after two months you should consider adding some extras, but in moderation. However, *do not* resume using credit; remember how you got overextended in the first place. If possible, pay off the accounts with the highest finance charges first, since those balances obviously are costing more in interest.

Consider setting aside some savings. The easiest way to save is through payroll deductions by your employer. It's easier when the money never passes through your hands. Or you can ask your bank to make an automatic transfer from your checking account to your savings account each month. Or try this: After you finish paying off a bill or a loan, continue making the payment—to your savings account. It is wise to keep money in savings equal to at least three-months' salary in order to meet emergencies.

The following is about two families who tried financial dieting and succeeded:

Louise, a single-parent schoolteacher, after three months on her financial diet plan, decided she could afford to resume having her hair fixed each week. She also began taking her three children out to eat twice a month, which they all enjoyed and appreciated more than when they ate out more often. But she firmly states, "I'll never let myself get into that shape again. And I'll never have another credit card!" (She destroyed all 12 of her plastic cards on the first day of her diet plan.)

Then there's Mike, a $40,000-a-year executive, and his wife Nancy, who vowed they would continue a regular savings plan, even after six months of strict dieting, which finally saw them current on all their unpaid bills. In addition, Mike added, "I'm going to join a car pool, the kids will be rewarded for turning off lights, and we're going to spend more time at home with the family instead of entertaining friends."

Isn't that neat?

Remember to include all members of the household in your financial diet plan—even the wee ones. The new shape of your finances can be just as exciting as the trim figure you gain from food dieting. Maybe you will want to initiate a financial diet plan and a fat diet plan at the same time. Keep good records on both so that you can chart your progress.

Getting in shape financially will include the need to *work*. Many people testify that God's provision has included the miracle of overtime, or of an opportunity to baby-sit some extra hours, or perhaps to fix a car or paint a house. If you are one of those people who think of work as a curse, I have news for you. Work is one of mankind's greatest satisfactions. The desire to be occupied with meaningful activity is built into our very being. Adam's life began in an enviable paradise, but his days were filled with both physical labor (tending the garden) and mental activity (naming the animals). The variety God built into Adam's days is a good balance for today's fast-paced world.

Provisions in the Garden of Eden were so plentiful that Adam and Eve's "work" was pure pleasure. Since the Fall, however, the human race has learned the meaning of laboring "by the sweat of the brow" for the basic necessities of food and shelter. Perhaps as you studied the various charts you were amazed to see what a large portion of your own life is spent working for these necessities.

Work, no matter what kind it may be, makes us appreciate our leisure time, while too much leisure generally results in boredom. Doing nothing wears a person out very quickly, as many who have been forced to slow down readily admit.

Work is honorable. God expects Christians to work, to

work hard, and to do a good job for God's glory. Many scriptures deal with work, and many others speak of the bad consequences of both laziness and "chasing fantasies." Working is part of God's plan for our lives and the penalty for not working is poverty and want.

On a television show I heard a man describe an unemployed person as one who

cannot find a job
at the wages he wants,
for the hours he wants,
doing the kind of work he wants.

The speaker was alluding to the fact that our system of compensating unemployed persons has made it possible for everyone to be selective in the type of work he does. Unemployment compensation payment for nonwork is a fairly recent phenomenon. Though it has been abused by some people, unemployment compensation as a means of helping a person during short periods of hardship represents a compassionate and generous act of sharing. Anyone who has experienced an extended enforced layoff appreciates both unemployment compensation and loving charity, which can come from many sources, including Christian friends or the church. Most unemployed people sigh for the day an employer chooses *them* from among the many applicants.

In a day when even employment bureaus have laid off help, we are aware of individuals who have done everything in their power to find work, without success. Nonetheless, Scripture admonishes us to be hard workers, doing something useful to help earn our own keep and a little extra to share with others in need. Even in our modern time we hear stories of believers who have humbled themselves before God, accepting jobs "beneath their dignity" and trusting Him to stretch that meager income to pay the bills. Idle hands are not pleasing to God. He expects us to provide for ourselves (*If a man will not work, he shall not eat* [2 Thess. 3:10]) and for our dependents (*If anyone does not provide for his immediate family, he has denied the faith and is worse than an unbeliever* [1 Tim. 5:8]).

As a rule, God does not hand out get-rich-quick schemes, nor does He drop showers of money on His faithful children. He grants us the blessing of strength for the day and the willingness to tackle jobs set before us, and He rewards us with a paycheck which we are responsible to use wisely.

If you are really committed to getting your finances in shape, you will succeed. Happiness is receiving your MasterCard statement marked "No balance due"!

Ralph Waldo Emerson understood that happiness and work are not always compatible when he wrote:

> The crowning fortune of a man is to be born to some pursuit which finds him employment and happiness, whether it be to make baskets, or broadswords, or canals, or statues, or songs.

But God can give you the ability to enjoy and even find happiness in your work—no matter how tiring or monotonous or demanding that work is. That we have the right attitude towards work is an important step in the direction of happiness. Our attitude should be that we are laboring for the sake of the Lord.

Now, get busy and put the ideas in this book to work for you along with your own fresh, new, creative ideas. Remember: Be original! Be innovative! It's *your* money plan and *you can* control how your money is spent. God is in your corner so stand on His promises.

> *Commit to the Lord whatever you do, and your plans will succeed* (Prov. 16:3).

But remember that money cannot buy happiness. It can bring happiness if other areas of our lives are in proper perspective and our priorities are straight, in other words, if we have put God first.

Reread chapters two and three that describe the worksheets that will be helpful to you. Get yourself a pad of columnar paper, an adding machine, and a comfortable place to work and dig in. But keep it *simple.*

God wants you to be a winner, so expect a miracle!

It's your money!

Appendix

Scripture References on Money Matters

A. **God Promises to Help**
Deut. 8:18; 28:2, 11-12
Prov. 3:5-6; 16:3, 9
John 16:24
1 Cor. 5:17
Jas. 1:17

B. **God Will Supply Our Needs**
Ps. 37:4, 25
Matt. 6:25, 33
Luke 12:22-31
John 16:24
Phil. 4:19

C. **God Promises Prosperity**
Deut. 8:18; 28:11; 29:9
Josh. 1:8
Ps. 1:1-3; 35:27; 37:4; 84:11
Prov. 3:9-10; 21:21; 28:20
Isa. 1:19
Mal. 3:10
Luke 6:38
2 Cor. 9:6
3 John 2

D. **You Can Believe God's Promises**
Ps. 24:1
Prov. 3:5-6; 16:3, 9
Jer. 33:3
Mark 11:24
Luke 11:9-10
Rom. 8:31
Gal. 3:29
Heb. 13:8

E. **Our Responsibility**

Prov. 3:5; 22:26-27; 30:7-9
Matt. 6:19-21, 24; 25:21
Luke 12:48
1 Cor. 4:2
Phil. 4:12
1 Tim. 6:8
Heb. 13:5
Jas. 4:13-15

F. **Giving and Sharing**

Exod. 25:1-2
Deut. 12:6
Prov. 11:24-25
Mal. 3:10
Matt. 5:23-24; 6:2-4
Luke 6:38
Acts 20:35
1 Cor. 16:1-2
2 Cor. 8:7; 9:6-7, 11
1 John 3:17

G. **The Tithe**

Gen. 28:22
Lev. 27:30, 32
Deut. 12:6
Mal. 3:10
Matt. 23:23

H. **Work**

Deut. 28:12
Eccles. 5:12, 18; 6:19
Prov. 10:4, 16; 14:23; 28:19
Eph. 4:28; 6:7
Col. 3:23-24
1 Thess. 4:11-12
2 Thess. 3:10-12
1 Tim. 5:8

I. **Credit and Debt**

2 Kings 4:1
Prov. 22:26-27
Matt. 18:23-25, 28-30
Rom. 13:8

J. **Taxes**

Matt. 22:17-21, 24-27
Rom. 13:6-7

K. **Consequences of Greed**

Prov. 28:22
Eccles. 5:10
Luke 12:15
1 Cor. 6:9-10
Col. 3:5
1 Tim. 6:9-10
Heb. 13:5

L. **How God Feels About Dishonesty**

Exod. 20:15
Lev. 19:13
Deut. 25:16
Prov. 13:11; 20:23
Mal. 3:8
Luke 16:10-12
1 Cor. 6:9-10
Eph. 4:28

M. **Is Poverty Your Own Fault?**

Prov. 10:4; 11:24; 13:18; 14:23; 17:16; 19:15; 20:13; 21:17; 22:16; 23:21; 24:33-34; 28:13, 19, 22

N. **Wealth**

Deut. 8:18
Ps. 48:10; 49:16-17; 49:20
Prov. 3:13-14; 11:4, 28; 28:11, 20; 30:7-9
Eccles. 2:26; 5:12
Matt. 16:26; 19:23-24

Mark 4:18-19
Luke 6:24
Luke 12:16-21
2 Cor. 9:11
1 Tim. 6:7, 9-10, 17
Jas. 1:10-11; 2:1-4; 5:1-3
Rev. 3:17